C000059248

How to Refinish Furniture

How to Refinish Furniture

H. W. Kuhn

Editorial advisor, British edition
Stanley Barras

Kaye & Ward. London

First published in the USA 1963
First published in Great Britain
by Kaye & Ward Ltd 1973

Copyright © 1963 Fawcett Publications, Inc
Copyright © Revised Edition 1973 Kaye & Ward Ltd

All Rights Reserved. No part of this publication may be
reproduced, stored in a retrieval system, or transmitted,
in any form, or by any means, electronic, mechanical,
photocopying, recording or otherwise, without the prior
permission of the copyright owner.

ISBN 0 7182 0944 3

All enquires and requests relevant to this title should be
sent to the publisher, Kaye & Ward Ltd, 21 New Street,
London EC2M 4NT, and not to the printer.

Filmset in Photon Times 10 pt. by
Richard Clay (The Chaucer Press), Ltd, Bungay, Suffolk
and printed in Great Britain by
Fletcher & Son, Ltd, Norwich

CONTENTS

Repairing Old Furniture   9

Basic Remodelling   18

Removing Old Finishes   27

Preparing The Surface   34

Colouring Wood   37

The Clear Finishes   50

The Painted Finishes   66

Specialty Finishes   105

Potpourri   125

CREDITS

Photography. While the photography was done by the author, it was Anthony Gatti, of Glendale, Arizona, whose professional skill, advice and processing made possible the photo phase of this book. Mr. Gatti, a prize winning portrait and animal photographer, custom processed all negatives.

Epoxy Technology. Information and the demonstrations illustrating use of the Epoxy resin 'glues' were provided by Kris Neville, Los Angeles, California. Mr. Neville, co-author of the leading technical book in the field, has made significant contributions to the technology.

Paintings and Sculpture. The works of the late American artist, Ray Boynton were used in several illustrations. Sculpture by Beryl Boynton, his wife, and a pioneer American metal sculptor in her own right, were made available most generously by Beryl Boynton, Apache Junction, Arizona.

Technical assistance in preparing and setting up projects to illustrate methods was provided by Daniel G. Kuhn, Los Angeles, California; Thomas J. Kuhn, Rialto, California.

Thanks also for the cooperation of others who submitted their furniture to processing and gave permission to photograph their projects in process and their hands at work as well. Particularly: Jim Harmon, Margie Gatti, Beryl Boynton, Kris Neville, Fredricka Tyus, Ron Haydock and Harry Merken.

The author is solely responsible for all information which appears in this book. All processes and methods have been derived from years of practical operation of finishing shops and research.

Materials recommended or 'criticized' have been exhaustively tested.

PUBLISHER'S NOTE

This book is a mine of practical information for the expert and the 'do it yourself' enthusiast. Success in any venture, such as is fully described under each section, depends upon obtaining suitable materials. Those detailed in this edition are the British equivalents of the materials mentioned in the American edition. They are obtainable in D.I.Y. shops, paint stores, wholesale suppliers to the trade and as a last resort from the firms advertised in the Yellow Pages Classified of your area.

Safety measures you must take are given in the appropriate sections of the book. They must be read before you start work for most of the materials are volatile and inflammable. Never work near an open fire, live electric bar fires or burning gas rings. Extinguish pilot lights. Read the section on the *Use of Spray Equipment* in 'The Clear Finishes'; the section *Dangers* under 'Colouring Wood', and note the stricture on the use of carbon tetrachloride in *Cleaning the Old Finish* under 'The Painted Finishes'. Finally, treat *all* processes and materials with the caution of the expert.

S.B.

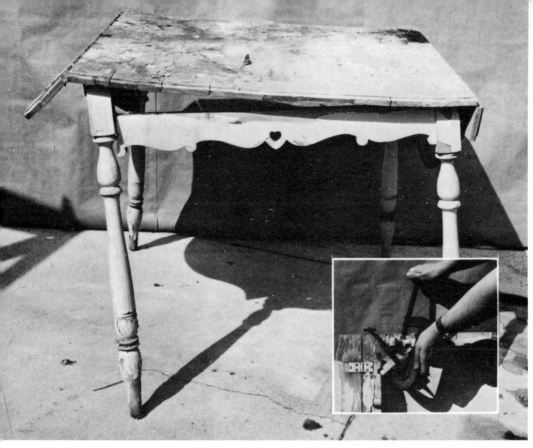

Be sure an old piece of furniture is worth fixing before you start the job. Table shown can be salvaged. Inset shows how small block and two G cramps are used to draw in one of the corner braces for gluing.

Repairing Old Furniture

BEFORE a piece of furniture is coloured and finished, visible surface flaws of all kinds must be corrected and the cabinet work must be made solid. Doors and drawers are fitted to work smoothly, the hardware is replaced if necessary and the wood surface which will support it is prepared to receive fastenings.

It would take a complete book to cover the many phases of furniture repair. Our concern is with the minor preparation necessary to put a reasonably sound piece in good condition.

You will do well to avoid buying or trying to rebuild any piece that requires extensive remodelling unless you are somewhat skilled in cabinet work.

Pieces that are to get a painted finish which will completely cover the wood or even coat it with a semi-opaque tone do not require the attention to detail about surface flaws that is necessary with pieces you will finish in clear coatings.

Perhaps the piece does not even require

9

stripping of the old finish if you are going to do it over in an antique white or a colour. But if you are going to strip the piece, some repairs should be made first and others are best done after the finish is removed.

Patching compounds like wood stopping or plastic wood and some glues are affected by the chemical action of paint remover. Paint remover shrewdly works its way into loose joints to prevent glue from getting to the wood surface and burrows down into small flaws which are difficult to clean out afterwards.

All loose joints and split boards should be reglued before stripping. Large flaws that you can easily scrape clean after stripping can be repaired then, but tiny flaws (such as nail holes) are best filled with wood stopping first, even though the remover will soften the surface. When the stripping is completed, you can scrape the top off the patch and resurface it.

Meanwhile, the hole has been kept free of remover and gunk. Remover softens paint, enamel, varnish and lacquer and turns all into a paste which we call gunk. A finish will not take over any gunk. Glue will not stick to gunk. If you want to be a good finisher, become a determined antigunker.

Tools and Materials

Common hand tools: A small cabinet saw; one or two small carving chisels; screw-driver; hammer; mallet; a nail set; wood rasp; small block plane (useful but not essential).

Finishing papers: Cabinet glass paper (not common sand paper which is much too coarse and inefficient). Papers ranging between Nos. $1\frac{1}{2}$–1–0–00. A coarse paper such as M2 can be used at times for rough shaping.

Glue: Any of the standard white glues now available in the plastic squeeze bottle dispenser. Any epoxy resin glue for joints that cannot be clamped, etc. Epoxy sets hard when thick and will fill loose joints, such as sockets for chair rungs. It binds firmly without any pressure.

You can fill minor flaws with a cellulose filler or a plastic wood filler and sand them smooth. Pick a colour which is close to the tone you'll have in the finish.

Grain is easy to simulate if plastic wood and cellulose filler are used in a large hole. In left-to-right sequence below, fine lines are scratched in the dried filler; then stain or filler is brushed on the spot and rubbed in; finally, the toned surface and the filled-in scratches blend in nicely.

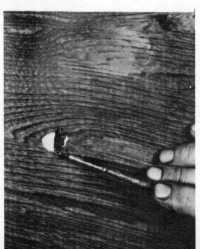

Repair materials: Plastic wood such as the Rawlplug product can build up broken carvings and smooth surfaces; cellulose filler such as Polyfilla is used to fill grain, holes and general depressions in surfaces; grain filler as marketed by Rustons fills cracks, depressions and wood grain prior to staining and finishing; Brummer stopping has been used for many years to fill nail holes and broken surfaces while the long established Alabastine can also be used on wood with good effect.

Pieces of veneer for patching depressions in surfaces, small chunks of wood for filling large flaws and reinforcing joined surfaces, such as a table top to the frame and small finishing nails, brads and screws are all brought to good use.

Cramps: Standard furniture or cabinet cramps. G cramps are fine. However, you can make simple cramping fixtures and one or two regular cramps can do.

The Repair Work

1. Surface flaws: These include gouges, scratches, burns, holes, chipped and loose veneer.

Plastic wood or stopping and a cellulose filler tinted to the proper tone to blend with the final finish are amazingly versatile materials which will suffice for nearly all the surface flaws. Use the first to nearly fill any larger depressions and the second for the small flaws and to top off the wood filler when used.

Clean out the depression throughly, cutting the hole larger if necessary to get to clean, solid wood. This is particularly important when you are cutting away the charred wood of a burn. Even when the edges of the hole look clean, there may be more char. To check it, wet the spot slightly with paint thinner or a turps substitute. This will show up any char faster than a fingerprint test will convict a three-year-old accused of raiding a sweet jar.

When the hole is completely clean, pack plastic wood (if the hole is so large it requires it) into it not more than $\frac{1}{4}$-inch thick. Let it dry completely so that it is as hard as wood before

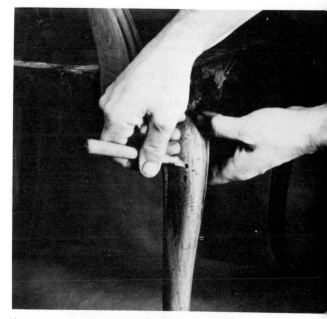

If there is a burn or gouge in fine furniture, you must first cut out the area that is charred or discoloured. A thin, sharp Exacto knife is good. Then a plastic wood is used.

building another layer. Applying plastic wood too thickly at one time will result in shrinkage and it will require much longer to harden.

Apply a cellulose filler with a small chisel, laying it in firmly and smoothly. You must leave the packing a little higher than the surrounding surface to permit fine sanding and compensate for some shrinkage.

To simulate wood grain in a surface-filled patch, scratch very fine little lines across it that will tie in with the real grain lines of the surrounding wood. Close examination of the grain of mahogany or walnut will reveal to you that what appear to be simply lines are actually small pits and grooves. If you use a magnifying glass, you will see the simplicity with which grain can be copied with a sharp-pointed little knife or carving chisel.

It is generally much easier to make the grain imitation this way than later with brush

11

strokes. The stain you use will darken the incised marks just as it does the real grain of the wood. A few marks are to be preferred to many. It takes only a very few small hairline scratches to create the impression of grain. Too many will be very obvious in the finished work.

As with all other methods in this book, experiment before you work on a piece you want to refinish. Experiment and practise on scrap wood.

Building up a carving or a moulding that has been chipped or chunked out is quite possible using only plastic wood and cellulose filler. After you have built up the spot with plastic wood to form a rough shape only, let it partially harden then wet the surface with the recommended solvent and use any small tool, such as a carving chisel, screw-driver, penknife or a little wood paddle, to shape the material as you might shape modelling clay. You can also use a brush and solvent to paint the built up surface into smooth shapes because the solvent softens the filler and forms a wet paste that can be handled almost like heavy paint.

You may well find that with smaller areas you are better served with a cellulose filler which does not contract away from the sides of the space to be filled.

When the repair is dry, complete the details of the shape by carving or brushing or once again delicately shaping with a tool and solvent, building small bits of filler as necessary.

Colour can be added to the repair as you are brushing it to shape with thinner or you can gently wipe colour over simpler forms with a small cloth pad dipped in colour and lacquer thinner. (Lacquer thinner is easily obtainable from motor accessory shops.) This is especially effective if you are repairing a tiny flaw on a finished piece and do not want to damage the surrounding finish while blending colour over the patch.

Nail holes, screw holes and the like may be darkened around their perimeters. Cut this away just as you would the charred area of a burn or it will show black through the final finish. Plug the hole by gluing in a piece of wood and top it off carefully with a suitable filler such as the ones already mentioned.

Large depressions such as those caused by big burns are best repaired with implanted wedges of wood that match the surface so that the grain and colour will be very close to the piece being repaired. Cut the hole slightly tapered and trim it to shape with straight-line cuts so that you can easily fit the wedge insert down into it. Drill a small hole in the bottom of the depression to let the glue have an escape area and permit you to press the block all the way down.

Make the repair piece thicker than necessary to fill the hole so that you can clamp it or hammer it down tightly and leave enough exposed above the surface of the repair to cut away and sand down smoothly. If the block doesn't fit perfectly, pack cellulose filler in the border after the piece is trimmed down and when you sand all will be well for you can scratch grain lines in.

Still another way to camouflage a large flaw is to inlay a piece of veneer of matching wood. This device works well, of course, where veneer has been torn away from surface, but it is also very good looking when used to top off a wedge repair such as we just described. In such a case, be sure the block of wood pressed into a hole—or the plastic wood packed into a hole—is perfectly smooth on top and levels off just a little lower than the surface. Check this out with a small piece of veneer which you can lay in the spot to see if it can be glued in place, leaving only a hair above the surrounding area for sanding.

From a sheet of veneer (or thin wood panelling about $\frac{1}{8}$ inch thick or less) select a grain pattern that will either blend in with the grain of the surface being repaired or appear natural, as would a knot, a pear shape or an irregular form. Do not use any straight cuts. An irregular, longer-than-wide leaf shape works well. After you cut it out, use it as a pattern, laying it over the repair spot. Scratch in the shape tightly, then carve out the shallow inlay area. Set the piece in this inlay area and glue it in place either by clamping, pressing with weights of any kind or tacking it down with fine little wire brads which you will remove after the glue is dry.

Now, even if this irregularly shaped patch does not fit as perfectly as you would like, it will look good when you fill the margins with plastic wood, for that filler will appear to be a part of the over-all pattern.

Loose veneer is simply glued down and pressed with weights or clamps. You may also be able to hot press loose veneer if the glue is water-solvent. The only way to find out is to wet the old glue and press the veneer with an electric iron. How hot? Experiment first and determine what setting your iron must have to cook the glue dry without charring the wood. This same technique can be used to press any piece of veneer if you use fresh glue with it (in place of clamping). But experiment first.

The joining edges of any spot repaired with veneer or a wood block will look better and fit tighter if you burnish the seams with a piece of smooth hardwood. Rub the burnishing stick over the joint, pressing the wood down and together before sanding.

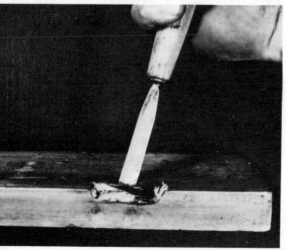

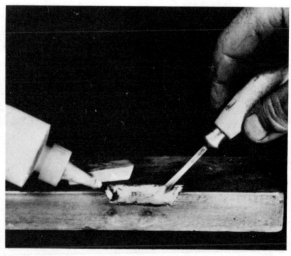

Left: Cross section of a deep burn in a wooden top which is to be repaired with a simple wedge insert. *Bottom left:* The charred area is carved away entirely and the hole is then shaped to a clean-edged rectangle with a sharp chisel. Note that the sides of the hole are tapered towards the bottom, though this is not necessary. *Bottom right:* A coat of white production glue is applied to the sides and bottom.

13

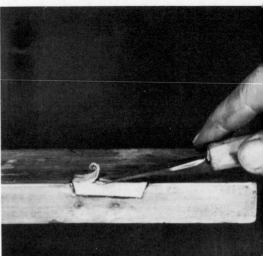

Repair of the deep burn is continued in the series on this page. *Top left:* Slightly tapered rectangular block of matching wood is driven into the hole with a mallet. *Top right:* Most of the excess of the block is cut away with a chisel. *Left:* After glue has dried, the edges around the block are filled in with coloured filler (unless you have managed a perfect fit). *Bottom left:* Sanding the surface to a smooth finish. *Below:* Final touch-up of patch with oil colour.

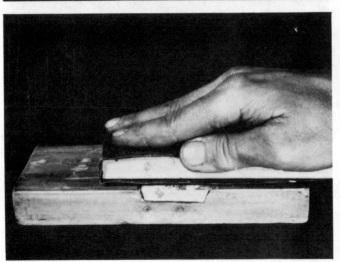

In place of a wedge block cut to shape, you can fill up a deep hole with a 'sandwich'. Glue in pieces of veneer or thin slabs of wood layer on layer, nailing them down with small finishing nails or brads. Pack plastic wood in the margin between the pieces and the sides of the hole. Then apply a sheet of veneer to the top as we described above—or top the work with cellulose filler and scratch-grain it.

Contact adhesive can be used to apply the veneer if you are not going to finish the piece with lacquer and if you have stripped the finish first. Lacquer thinner dissolves contact adhesive.

Apply adhesive to the sides to be bonded as per instructions on the container. Set the veneer piece in place and press firmly, rubbing it with a hardwood block; then burnish in the edges. This will give you an 'invisible' repair if you taper the edges of the veneer and the edges of the hole enough so that when you press the veneer in place you can burnish off the tapered edge into the wood surface surrounding—and if you select a piece with matching grain!

2. Splits, large cracks and separated pieces: Where possible, of course, rejoin separated pieces by gluing and clamping them together. But where clamping is impractical, such as on a chest top that has a large shrinkage opening in it, thin slices of wood (splines) are inserted with glue and driven in tightly.

For large openings such as result from extraordinary shrinkage of some wood, cut a piece of wood (same kind if to be finished clear) that fits the opening closely. It is best to cut the piece a little oversize in width so that you can taper it just a little towards the bottom. Apply glue to the joining edges and press the spline into the opening. Pressure applied by clamps is best—or drive the piece in with gentle taps of a mallet, using a block of wood under the mallet to avoid cracking or mashing the spline.

For smaller separations, wedge strips of veneer into the opening in the same manner as a spline. It is not necessary to clamp these, however. Simply push them in place and drive in the tighter-fitting strips.

When the glue has set completely (4–12 hours) then fill the remaining openings with slivers, pieces of wood or veneer after applying glue to them. Fill remaining openings and pits with wood cellulose filler just as you will any other small flaws.

The reverse sides of panels can be given extra strength where needed by gluing a flat, smooth plate of wood (about $\frac{1}{8}$ inch or $\frac{1}{4}$ inch thick) across the joint or gluing supporting strips of wood there. Apply these after smoothing off the spline that fills the opening.

3. Firming up the frame: The framework supporting a table must be solid and the top securely fastened to it to prevent wobbling. If screws holding a table top or chest top are loose and cannot be tightened, stuff the screw holes with slivers of wood and glue. Little blocks of wood glued to the underside of tops and sides of cabinets at the framework corners will give added rigidity.

Apply glue to the back or bottom panel of a cabinet before renailing it to the frame. Use glue wherever possible for added strength, even if the parts were nailed or screwed together before.

A cabinet whose bottom is rotted or otherwise unable to hold the piece solidly should be replaced or simply covered over with a new sheet of plywood and the legs reset accordingly. Supply a cabinet with a firmly glued back and base and all will be well. Most long cabinets which are shaky need the back (often of hardboard or Masonite or a thin sheet of plywood) glued and nailed more tightly to the frame.

4. Doors and drawers: Fit doors by planing off their edges as necessary after stripping. Remember that a painted finish in particular adds a little to the size of the door. Glue up loose drawers and do any sanding or planing necessary to insure a smooth sliding fit. If you need a lubricant on them, solid soap or candle wax works well.

5. Socket joints: If you can draw the leg or rung out of its socket, do so. Clean the old glue off and reset the piece with glue. Use slivers of wood for wedges if necessary. When you cannot separate the rung from its socket enough to clean out the old glue, drive slim wedges of hardwood (with glue applied) into the socket. When the glue has dried, pack the joint with plastic wood.

6. Loose framing joints: Tenon fittings and dowel fittings often cannot be separated and the best you can do is to work glue into the joint with a thin piece of tin, wiggling the joint as you do so.

Wherever possible, open the joint a little with a chisel and scrape off the old glue. If there is dirt or remover or gunk in the joints, flush it out with lacquer thinner. Moderate pressure applied to the joining members after gluing will always help. If you do not have cramps, or cannot rig up a clamp fixture, use rope or a strap to bind the joint. Even heavy rubber bands cut from old inner tubes will help.

Where they will not harm the surface, nails and screws can be used to good effect in strengthening loose joints.

Drilling a small hole where it will not show on the surface, but where it will extend into a joint (such as the fitting of a standard leg to a chair frame) and then squeezing glue into the opening until it shows around the joint is a fine way to stiffen up such joints.

7. Epoxy resins: These relatively new 'glues' solve many problems. The resin and hardening agent come in separate tubes for each measuring before mixing. Unlike other glues, epoxy is strong and holds well when it sets up in an open joint. Most glues are strong only with a tight joint bonded by a thin glue application. Epoxy resin will not bind any joint that is oily, greasy, waxy or dirty. It will bind the dirt or grease together, but not the wood. Clean out a joint with lacquer thinner. If you have to, drill a hole and use an eye dropper to force the thinner into the joint.

Follow directions on the epoxy tubes closely

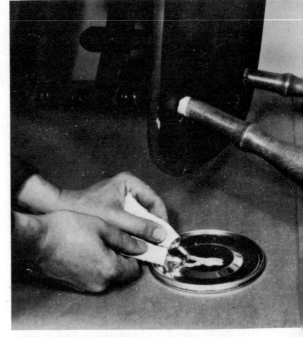

One problem which often occurs is the loosening of chair legs or rungs. A lasting repair can be made by using the newer epoxy resin, a two-part cement. (Araldite is a well-known make.) The resin and a catalyst, sold in tubes, must be mixed as shown.

and force the cement into joints or simply pack it in where possible. No clamping is necessary afterwards, but the piece must set several hours without disturbing the joint.

8. Miscellaneous notes: Pieces to be painted or ghesso-coated can be repaired like an old box. Use nails, screws and whatever so long as the surfaces are then covered with cellulose filler to produce a smooth area.

Where a natural finish is to be applied, avoid driving nails or screws through observable areas. Very many wood filled and plastic wood patches will disfigure the piece by showing through the clear finishes.

A piece that requires a great deal of surface repair and patching or sanding is best finished

16

in one of the painted or semi-painted finishes. Do not attempt to make a fine finished surface on such a piece. If necessary, remodel it with veneer or a plastic laminate such as Formica.

Use of any wipe-in crayon-type fillers, dry powder grain filler, spackle, etc., is undesirable and usually tragic. The only way to be successful is to be firm. With the thousands of varied products on the market to make it 'easy' for you, your only hope is to resist all temptation and stick with the materials listed.

Veneered surface of piece at left was burned through, but veneer of similar grain pattern can be patched into the area. Irregular piece is cut first and is made to extend to the edge if the damage is reasonably close. Lower left photo shows patch being used to outline the damaged area. Below, wooden plate beneath clamp serves to protect surface of the piece.

17

Basic Remodelling

HERE again, as with the repair work, are only some very basic ideas to guide you. Remodelling extensively is properly a matter of cabinetry, not refinishing. But often a new top for a chest or the addition or removal of moulding, carving and other gingerbread or a slight alteration in height may make the big difference between an average clunker and a thing of beauty.

New hardware can make a great improvement in many pieces. Select good quality handles and fittings.

Use your own good artistic judgment. Look long and well at the piece. Visualize it changed. What happens if the little rosettes are taken off? If the fancy curlicues are cut off? If it could be made a little taller or shorter by changing legs? If a piece of trim is added here or there? If arms are removed from chairs? If two drawers are converted into a door space?

Trim, moulding and appliqués are available through several mail order houses and at lumber mills, cabinet shops and stores catering for hobbyists. Other pieces of junk furniture can yield an abundance of parts for remodelling.

Remove old trim carefully· Check first to see if it is applied with nails, screws or just glue and dowels. Remove nails and screws and cut off a little at a time to avoid splitting the surface under the trim.

Apply new trim with glue and use small brads to hold the pieces in place until the glue dries. Otherwise, use clamps, weights, etc.

Chests can be lowered by cutting them off at one of the drawer separators where the framework supporting a drawer will be the frame to which you can glue and screw the top.

You can remove a couple of drawers from a chest and substitute doors to make a cabinet.

Commodes can be converted to Hi-Fi and record cabinets by removing the tops and mounting properly fitted supports or shelves inside the piece. Remove the top drawers that would interfere with the support and after taking the drawer fronts off the drawers, reset the drawer fronts in place for appearance (false drawers) by gluing with wedges around all sides.

The most common problem in remodelling relates to tops of chests or tables that are too far gone to be repaired easily. A complete new top of plywood or solid wood is quite easy to install on some pieces where it is a matter of removing holding screws and a few glue blocks. The new top is then secured in the original manner.

A second method, most applicable where removal of the old top would involve considerable skill and work, is to apply a new surface to the old top, either wood or a synthetic such as Formica. In either case, level off and smooth the old surface by sanding or planing. Fill the heavy flaws and repair splits enough to provide a good solid base for the new surface sheet.

A sheet of thin plywood with the top side made of wood that matches the piece is the simplest laminate, since it is reasonably rigid and offers no difficulty in smooth application. Where possible, use one solid sheet cut a fraction of an inch larger than the surface. Apply Contact Adhesive to each surface to be bonded and, when it has set up as per instructions on container, press the plywood firmly in place and weight it down or clamp it lightly.

If a joint has become loose, spread the pieces apart with a chisel and scrape the edges clean.

A warped board can be cut halfway through with a hacksaw blade. Use straight rail as a guide.

Contact Adhesive holds on contact. You cannot shift the piece around after placing it. Therefore, to insure an accurate placement, mount a stop on one end of the top being covered. When you put the veneer in place on edge against the stop, accurate position is obtained.

A level, smooth surface makes for a perfect bond. You can hammer the sheet down, using a large block of wood to prevent damage from the hammer, but clamping it with the aid of several lengths of 2 × 4 or 1-inch trim stock across the top is best. If you have enough clamps or weights, and the top is very smooth, you can use a white glue in place of the Contact Adhesive. This must dry at least 12 hours before you finish the surface.

Do not attempt to bond a new top on to a painted or otherwise finished surface. Clean off the old top by scraping or sanding.

To finish the raw edge of plywood, first sand it down with a sanding block. Fill the porous edge with plastic wood and sand it when dry. The entire exposed edge (old and new top) can also be covered with a veneer border (available

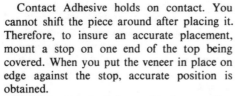

Thin spline (coated with white glue) is driven in after warped board is glued and nailed down.

20

The glued boards should be drawn together with a long clamp or clamps to ensure a solid joint.

Good 'T' clamps are easily glued up and nailed. Use flat-head bolts to hold the pivoting blocks.

in ready-to-apply strips) or thin strips of wood. Glue these and set them in place with small finishing nails.

You must have a perfectly smooth surface to apply veneer properly. Do not attempt it on large cabinets or tables, but on small coffee tables, commodes and chests it is not too difficult. You probably cannot obtain a sheet of veneer wide enough for the top. Cut two pieces to match with clean joining edges. Tape them together to hold them as one piece. To the top of this prepared sheet, place tape around all the edges to prevent splitting. Apply it in the same way as the plywood, laying the veneer at one end first, then pressing it down to the surface. A paint roller can be used to press it well and it should be pounded a little with hammer and block to set it perfectly.

Before applying any new top, use a coarse sandpaper under a large block to level the surface.

Chisel off the exposed part of the spline after joint has set up hard (from two to four hours).

Plane the boards down flush where you have had to level off a warp or fix a joint with a spline.

Cut new top (plywood in this case) to size and apply it with brads and glue or contact adhesive.

Mouldings of various types are available at lumber dealers for finishing of raw plywood edges.

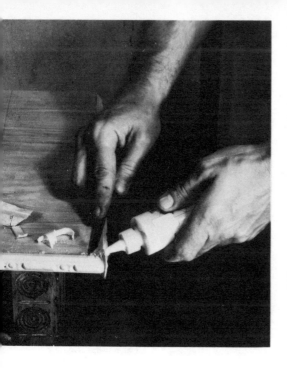

Above left: When you have mitred the corners of trim and the job is less than perfect, fill in with a glue and sawdust mix or put plastic wood into voids.

Above: Whenever it is desirable to cover a flaw or any unwanted design, you can use a strip of matching veneer. Clean the area, then sand thoroughly.

Left: Concealing some designs on the chest with strips of Woodtape. The paper backing is removed and a cement solvent is applied to hold strips.

23

Above left: Veneer strips may not match the old wood exactly, but they can be toned with colouring later.

Above: If you have to mould plastic wood, do it with a chisel or cloth pad wet with the recommended solvent.

Left: These doors could not be removed easily but the edges were trimmed with a plane for a snug fit.

Opposite page: Backing is peeled from veneer strip which will hide scratched drawer front and old knob holes.

Top right: Guide rails nailed to cabinet sides aid in accurate placement of Formica on Contact Adhesive.

Below left: A cloth pad, a block of wood and a mallet will do to hammer the Formica out flat if necessary.

Below right: Using lap-joint trim, available at lumberyards, is the easiest way to finish off Formica edges.

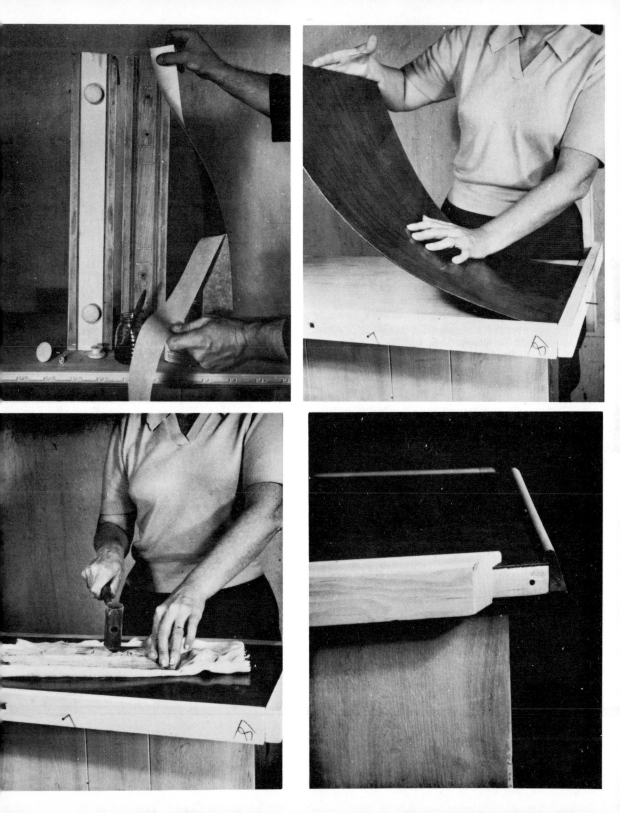

Note: Lacquer thinner and lacquer will dissolve Contract Adhesive. Therefore, do not apply a lacquer finish over this veneer, but use another type such as oil-resin or varnish.

If any blisters develop in the veneer that you cannot press out evenly, cut them open with a razor blade, using a cross-cut, and trim the pie-wedge sections down on their edges so they can be pressed flat.

Plastic laminates are applied like plywood, using either the Contact Adhesive or the mastic type used to lay tile or ceramics.

The laminate is extremely difficult to cut or work down for smooth edges; therefore, have the sheet cut accurately. A good idea is to have it cut for you a fraction of an inch smaller than the top so you can sand or plane the wood edge down to the size of the laminate. Edge banding is applied as trim or aluminium trim can be set over the edges on cabinets that do not require the finished wood look of fine furniture.

In many cases—particularly small tables—a new top of marble or brecchia or synthetic stone is the ideal solution. These are either laid on the top or cemented with mastic bonding cement. Also, blocks of ceramic tile or mosaics produce beautiful effects and can make a junker into a piece of fine furniture.

Ready-made legs with easy-to-apply metal fastenings are now available generally. Wrought iron type legs also are in supply. These, together with sheets of plywood having one good side of walnut, mahogany, teak or another fine furniture wood, make good-looking utility tables and benches or can be used to give an old piece of cabinetry a truly new look.

Remember that many pieces in such rough surface condition that they seem to call for new tops or panels may look even better if you refinish them with paint after patching up the surface.

You can also apply any of several kinds of coverings to achieve interesting results. Decorator burlap cemented to an otherwise plain, boxy cabinet can look well. Picture wallpaper, tapestry, solid colour papers, clothes, almost anything that you can cement to a coffee table top and cover with a sheet of plate glass can turn a clunker into a conversation piece.

Ghesso covers many flaws. If you repair a piece of cabinetry well and then cover its surfaces with thin sheets of plywood, veneer, Masonite or even heavy cardboard, you can then coat this surface with ghesso or with solid colour finishes such as enamel. But only if you make the cabinet rigid and apply the sheets securely and smoothly will you accomplish anything worth while.

Removing Old Finishes

'THERE, but for the atrocious mess of removing old paint or varnishes, is a beautiful piece of furniture I'd love to refinish!'

This is the mournful cry of all too many frustrated refinishers. But stripping off old finishes is easy and can be clean work. No matter how ghastly your past experience in this very necessary and painless operation, have faith in your ability to do the job well.

You can strip any kind of finish off any piece of furniture in your best suit and not get a drop on it or your hands. It is easier still if you do not mind getting your hands a little dirty or wear rubber gloves. Note to the ladies: Don't overdo this faith thing. Paint removers are deadly enemies of nylon and other synthetic fabrics as well as soft, delicate skin. Refuse to

let anyone tell you how they or their Aunt Fanny used to do it. Do not give in to the persuasive sales talk of your favourite paint shop dealer. Do it in the following manner and you will not go wrong.

Tools and Materials for Stripping

The kind (not brand) of remover you use is extremely important. In any town where there is a shop catering for finishers (not painters) you can buy a professional-type liquid remover. Another source is a store that supplies automotive refinishers with their products. These removers are far less costly than the many varieties sold almost exclusively in retail stores to the nonprofessional. A good remover is liquid and requires no neutralizing solution.

Buy some 4-0 and 3-0 steel wool. An excellent new product on the market much better than steel wool is the Scotch Pad, similar to a scouring pad. It will not scratch the wood and will not fall apart. It can be used over and over again. It is the answer to the stripper's prayer.

You will need some cheap bristle brushes. Do not use synthetics. Brushes of 1–3 inches work well. Get a flexible putty knife with an edge not very sharp to avoid scratching. Check the corners of the edge and file away any sharpness that might scratch. Some old tins are required. Coffee tins are ideal. Also provide a metal container for the gunk. Lots of cotton rags are also needed. Avoid silk, nylon and slick materials that are not absorbent.

Spread several layers of newspaper where you are going to work. It holds the slop quite well without soaking through.

You will work with remover and lacquer thinner. Pour this from the containers into tin cans large enough to leave ample room at the top to avoid spilling. Set a large fruit juice tin inside a coffee tin or gallon can to avoid all dripping and to hold your brush.

Stripping. Plan on working one piece at a time. Do not attempt all the drawers of a five-drawer chest, the dresser and the bed of a set, for example. Start with a small piece and then learn your pace.

Lay out flat pieces on supports. Put chests, tables and chairs on pieces of wood. An excellent method is to set a block of wood inside a flat pan or coffee tin to support each leg. This can will collect the drippings.

Let us presume we are doing a chest. We will work on it with the drawers removed. Apply the remover with a brush to the top of the chest. Do not paint it on! Lay it on in gentle, no-splash, short strokes. Lay it on the sides of the chest by stroking across the side, starting at the top. Try to avoid putting it on so heavily that it runs.

After covering the entire chest this way, wait five or ten minutes until you can see and test (by dragging the brush over the finish) that

The first step, before stripping the old finish off furniture, is to take off all the hardware.

A roll of paper in each hardware hole prevents any of the remover from dripping into a drawer.

Paint skin, not at all messy, builds up on the putty knife. Entire piece is stripped this way.

With a brush, more of the remover is applied to the surface and scrubbed lightly over the wood.

Use some 3-0 or 4-0 steel wool to rub off the stubborn spots that your soft brush didn't get.

Wipe down the wood with lacquer thinner to remove the last traces of both paint and remover.

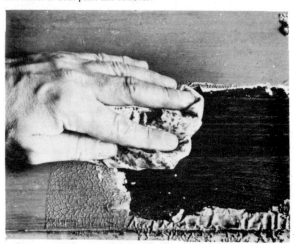

the remover has begun to work into the finish. Try not to rush the job.

Now, since it will soak up the remover, lay on a heavier application. Let this rest in peace without your help while it dissolves the old finish. The heavier the finish the longer it will take and the more applications will be required.

Continue to apply remover at regular intervals as long as the old finish is soaking it up. It will appear to dry out a little and lose its sheen as the remover soaks in and the finish will not slip off when you brush more remover on.

29

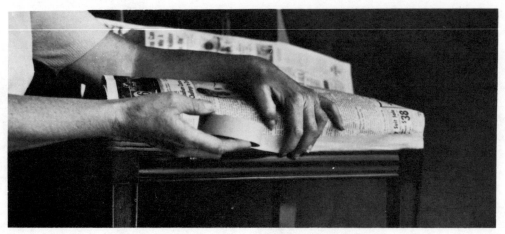

Before you start to strip the paint from any upholstered furniture, mask off the fabric very carefully.

When the finish does come off as you brush more remover on and the raw wood is revealed, then you are getting warm.

Try the finish with the putty knife. If the knife lifts the entire mass of finish cleanly from the wood, just keep on pushing the old slop off the top towards one end. Go over the entire top this way like shovelling snow and then push it off into a can. Do not use rags.

Push it down the sides in like manner. Use a small bristle brush (no splatter) to push it down the moulding and out of carvings, etc. A slow, steady pushing action is the trick. Do not scrub or splash as if you were mopping a garage floor.

Most varnish, lacquer and other similar finishes will come off easily this way. Old varnish requires much more soaking than newer finishes. But you add to the work by scraping away until the entire finish comes off. It may act like taffy, or wrinkle up in a sheet, or more or less flow off. If you run into a thin, rather modern lacquer finish it may brush off without any need for using the putty knife. Many pieces can be completely stripped in this way, using only a brush and never even wetting your hands.

Paints and enamels are usually harder to work than the clear furniture finishes. They must soak and soak and soak, depending on the number of coats on the piece.

Flushing the gunk. Use the remover with the brush and push off the gunk with a putty knife. Then use the brush to gently scrub with the remover in light circular motions. Follow this by using the brush with lacquer thinner to gently scrub off the residual gunk.

Next use the Scotch Pad or steel wool, dipping it in lacquer thinner if necessary to scrub away stubborn spots or a slick part that means the old finish is still clinging in a film to the wood.

Follow by washing the piece down thoroughly with a rag soaked in lacquer thinner. Scrub out crevices with a small brush and lacquer thinner; then wipe down with dry cloth. Afterwards, any spots missed can be cleaned by applying remover and scrubbing with steel wool or (where it will not damage the piece) by scraping or sanding.

Note: There are a few synthetic finishes that defy most liquid removers. If you run into a hard finish that will not dissolve at all, just forget it. Some of the modern plastic finishes will not come off with a pickaxe. Only sanding with power equipment when you have a weekend to waste will do the job. Just plan on painting the piece right over the old finish.

Any piece that is going to get a painted finish can be treated more roughly than one getting a clear finish. Scraping or sanding off the old finishes works well enough, but remember that in most cases it is not necessary at all to remove a finish that is going to have paint over it.

Never scrape an antique. Never sand the finish off an antique. Scraping any fine wood to be clear-finished is a risky operation which is strictly avoided by professionals. If the piece must be stripped and you do not want to do it—or cannot—then why not let a local company strip it for you? In larger cities this work is a highly specialized industry and the prices are very reasonable.

Clean up all waste and slop and dispose of it in metal containers. Wash brushes and tools in lacquer thinner. If you have worked with bare hands, wash with lacquer thinner and then with a bland soap.

CAUTION: Removers will eat through most cloth. Old clothes and shoes are the mark of wisdom until you have mastered this phase of the work. Then wear old clothes and old shoes anyhow (but knowing you don't really have to). Do not smoke while performing this operation. Avoid prolonged breathing of vapours. Work in an open garage or outside in the shade.

General hints: Use of any small metal tank in which you can place all or part of the work is the professional way. A simple tank can be made by nailing up 2 × 4's in a rectangular frame to the size wanted and wrapping thin sheet metal around it. No soldering is necessary. Use metal drums or cans to clean small

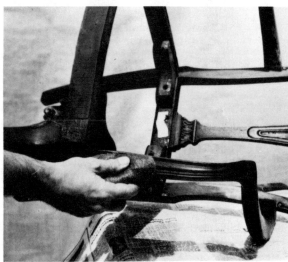

Left: If doing a chair, set each leg on a small can inside a bigger can and scrub the paint off with a brush after applying remover. *Above:* The hard-to-strip areas must be scrubbed well with steel wool. Wear gloves if hands are sensitive.

31

Flush all grooves with lacquer thinner and scrub them well with a brush to remove the gunk after a stripping process.

parts such as handles, soaking them in thinner.

When you wash down table legs, set them in cans and flush the remover down the leg liberally with a brush. Follow with other operations as necessary.

Always wipe down a surface with a rag after working to avoid stains resulting from the remover and thinner dissolving some of the stain in the wood and spreading in streaks.

When you have a table leaf that must be stripped on both sides or a desk drop-leaf, for example, strip the underside first and wipe it clean. Set it on clean wood blocks and do the top side. Follow up by wiping down both sides throughly to eliminate runs on the underside.

Where you have masked off glass, remove the masking tape immediately after washing down the wood and wipe any residue from the glass. It is necessary (without any way of getting out of it) to replace the masking tape for the finishing operations because the tape gets soaked with gunk and will ruin the finishing if left on. Do not try to use gummed paper or sellotape instead of masking tape.

Mask off brass ferrules on legs with tape and remove and replace masking before finishing.

Mask off sides of drawers and insides of drawers in desks you do not wish to damage with runs and streaks.

Mask off all glass to protect it and avoid extra cleaning when you have to refinish a piece. It is still better to remove the glass entirely.

Since you work the drawers with the front turned up (like a table top), plug the screw or hardware holes with wads of paper from the inside to avoid gunk running through. Be sure to plug the keyholes, also.

Chairs, especially windsors and the like are the most difficult of all. If you must remove the finish, then work from the top down and use a Scotch Pad or steel wool to scrub the softened finish off. Work is easiest in a tank in which you can lay the chair down on any side and let it soak in remover poured into the tank. You can then brush the finish directly into the tank, working this way until the piece is clean. Follow by flushing it with thinner.

If you are desperate and frustrated but bull-headed when a chair will not yield up its skin of five or six layers of paint and enamel, then secure a large enough drum to hold the chair and immerse the miserable thing up to its ears in remover. By swishing it up and down, the skin will fall off.

Stone cutters and various other commercial industries will often sandblast for you. Larger cities offer special sandblast service for wood. Light, proper sandblasting will remove the toughest finish from most furniture without seriously damaging the piece if it is hardwood. This is especially useful on oak.

Don't waste time trying to remove heavy, old paint and enamel finishes from pieces of furniture that are not of exceptional value. When you go bargain hunting, take a sharp little scraper (a carving chisel) with you and cut away on an underside to see how many layers of paint there are. When you see three or four colours and the finish is rock-hard, do not buy it for clear finishing. Plan on a painted finish or none.

If you want to strip the legs and arms of an upholstered piece, mask off the fabric carefully, set a leg in a coffee tin of remover and carefully brush the old finish off with the liquid. Wooden arms around cloth must be stripped carefully. Take great care to mask throughly and push the masking material down around the wood where it meets the fabric. Remove all masking at once after stripping.

Paste removers which cling to vertical surfaces can be used to good effect as a first application to sides of pieces, but are costly and not necessary.

When in doubt about securing the kind of industrial type remover recommended, go to your nearest refinisher and find out what he uses.

Stripping Guide List

1. Disassemble and spread pieces out in ample work space. Remove hardware.

2. Mask off glass, brass and any areas not to be stripped. Plug keyholes and other openings to avoid dripping.

3. Wearing rubber gloves and old clothes, pour lacquer thinner into a can and the liquid remover into another can. Close the containers.

4. Apply remover to surfaces, working no more surface than you can manage without having them dry up on you.

5. Let the remover soak in. Apply more as necessary.

6. When a putty knife can lift off the softened gunk, push the gunk off. Do not scrub with rags.

7. Scrub off last of finish gently with a brush. Then scrub with thinner.

8. Wipe down with a rag wet with lacquer thinner, then a dry rag.

9. Dispose of slop in metal containers.

Preparing the Surface

WHETHER it is a piece you have repaired, an unfinished piece you have bought or one you have built of good wood, so long as it has no finish to remove, preparation of the wood for the finish consists mainly of fine sanding.

Sanding good wood is one of the real pleasures of furniture work. Each wood has its distinctive aroma and feel, and as you work the surface down with finer and finer papers you will throughly enjoy the smooth sleekness of the wood and the basic beauty as the quality of the piece is revealed. Old cherry with its powder-like dust and sweet aroma is my personal favourite. But it is the feel of that unfinished wood that is the first reward for your work.

Sanding is done with *cabinet finishing papers* only. Work progressively to finer papers after beginning with paper no coarser than necessary to eliminate tool marks, fine scratches and the marks left from repair. Usually, this means beginning with a No. $1\frac{1}{2}$ paper and moving towards finer papers with No. 1 and No. 0. That is as fine as we ordinarily work, but since you are working for pleasure and for that custom, hand finish that even the most expensive pieces seldom get, go on to 00. Then use the finest papers of the Tri-M-Ite wet or dry line ordinarily used only on finishes: No. 400 first and No. 600 for the last perfect touch of the master. This produces so fine a surface

Sanding for a fine finish applies to areas that are hidden as well as exposed. Don't forget to do the undersides of chair arms for professional touch.

When refinishing drawers, always sand down sides to clean them and spray on a lacquer sealer from an aerosol can to protect wood.

that the wood is as smooth as though it were coated.

Note: Each finer paper in the series is designed to remove the lines produced by the cutting action of the abrasive particles on the paper used previously in number order. Sand in the direction of the grain with the papers running from F2 to 00. The finer papers can be used across the grain where absolutely necessary. Do not use any real pressure. The papers are designed to cut by a simple process of movement under minimal pressure.

Pieces to be finished clear will be only as beautiful and masterfully done as the sanding. Every extra stroke of fine paper that removes the smallest cross-grain scratch, every minute of additional time invested in sure straight passes with the grain to eliminate all marks

except those of the finest paper as seen under a magnifying glass will be the determining factor in the quality of your work. No piece is any better than its preparation.

Anyone can apply a finish, but dedicated artists and craftsmen take the time to sand, sand and sand until the surface is flawless, just as they must polish certain finishes until flawless. No matter how much work goes into the clear finish over wood that has scratches or inferior, labour-saving sanding, it can never look good.

Can you sand straight? It's quite a challenge to make your arm follow a straight line—one of the few frontiers for modern man to whip. It is like ironing, only much more rewarding.

Joints you have reglued or spots you have filled with wood splines or chips will seal tightly and look like flawless matched inlays when you burnish the joint. Do this before the finer sanding. Take a piece of hard wood such as maple or birch. Smooth it off to make a surface like a pad. Press it over the area as if ironing until it makes the wood shine. This compresses the wood and forces it to mash together.

Check and examine the piece as you sand. Patch remaining minor flaws with plastic wood. Very small patches of this kind will dry almost at once and while you are sanding another area will set hard.

For that final artistic touch for clear finishes (after the final finish sanding), rub down the wood with a pad made of unfinished, unstained leather wrapped around a block. Rub hard until the wood is warm. This burnishing presses out fine lines and hardens the surface to produce an unexcelled wood surface.

If you have a lathe and are working with maple or birch turnings, you can finish the turning by burnishing carefully with leather or flannel. Be careful not to burn or char the wood. Done to the right degree, this produces an amber tone and hard finish that gives a transparent appearance to the wood surface. This is followed by burnishing a mixture of one part varnish and three parts thinner into wood until dry.

Pieces to be painted

If stripped of its old finish, a piece to be painted does not require the fine sanding so necessary to those pieces that will receive a clear coating. However, the surface must be smooth. Following the repair work and the patching, sand the surfaces with F2 cabinet paper until you achieve an unpitted, even surface that will take the paint coating smoothly.

The scratches for paper coarser than F2 will show through most paint coatings. Indeed, it is best to follow up the F2 paper with No. 1 to be sure you leave no scratches.

If you are going to paint over an old finish, after repairing the piece and cleaning it of any wax or grease or dirt, then you should sand it with F2 and No. 1 just as you do the raw wood pieces.

Colouring Wood

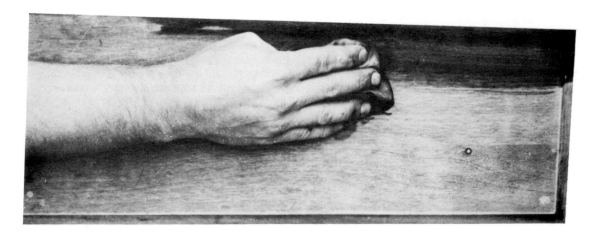

COLOURING the wood is essential to good finishing. Even the so-called 'natural wood' finishes incorporate some colouring of the wood to bring out the beauty of grain and emphasize the tone of the wood. The principle is much the same as in the use of cosmetics. Properly applied, make-up enhances the beauty of a woman's face. Overdone, it destroys the natural look and presents an artificial appearance.

The most subtle colourings are used on natural woods for this purpose. But colour then ranges through semi-transparent tones to conceal irregularities and poor grain or make several pieces of different wood look the same to solid-coloured finishes such as antique white, Chinese red or ebony.

While the methods of applying colour to the wood (as in staining or toning) and to the finish (as in glazing and shading) and over wood or finish (as in painting, enamelling or lacquering solid colour) vary slightly to achieve proper results, the basic principle of mixing colour and preparing a vehicle (solvent solution) for that colour are the same. Once you have grasped the ideas underlying preparation of the few colours used in furniture work, you can then experiment and create tones, stains and shades to please your own taste.

We will learn the transparent colourings first and deal with the opaque in a later chapter on painted finishes.

In our system of finishing, the basic colouring vehicle is paint thinner. To this is added oil tinting colours or brand-named tinting colours which are much better than the oil. They mix easier, dry faster and are less expensive. Boiled linseed oil is used to give the mixture a drying, sticking characteristic so it will not wipe off or be dissolved when the finish is applied. In some cases we will use a little varnish to give even tougher sticking qualities to the colours. The colouring will be done with brushes and lint-free rags (cotton is best). A spray gun or aerosol can can be used for certain of these operations. But let's understand some terms first:

Staining: Applying colour directly to the wood, to soak into the wood and not cover the grain in any way. This is much like dyeing cloth.

Colour toning: Applying colour to the wood (usually after staining) to blend the tone desired evenly, despite variation in the wood pieces or sections, and to compensate over areas that are bleached, faded or discoloured· This is like using pancake make-up over skin flaws. The grain is not concealed, but we simply do not let the wood soak up what it wants to; we control the colour shade and intensity by applying the tone and intensity we need.

Glazing: Transparent films of colour are applied over a finish to subtly alter the tone, like placing a tinted sheet of cellophane over a surface. We can darken, lighten or slightly alter the colour this way. Glazing as applied to solid colour finishes (as in antique white) means brushing off colour to reproduce little lines like grain and will be discussed in the section on painted finishes. Glazing to create real grain effects and other patterns is beyond the scope of the non-professional and will be merely

mentioned here. It requires great skill and experience.

Shading: Though similar to glazing a transparent film over a finish, shading is the application of darker (shadow) tones to corners, carvings or legs to achieve a stronger contrast of colours in the piece. Shading also means spraying a transparent darker tone over a finish to either darken it, even out the colour or shadow some areas.

Pigments: The oil colours or tinting colours.

Vehicle: The solution in which the pigment is mixed.

Milking: Adding white to a colour or colour mixture to lighten it.

The oil system: The process of finishing with any and all materials that are solvent in paint thinner, turpentine or oil, as distinguished from the lacquer system and the shellac system.

Dangers: Oil system materials are safe to use since they are not generally toxic, and will not normally cause rash or other skin problems. Their vapours are inflammable and open flames should be avoided when working with them. Do not heat these materials. Most dangerous are rags in which solutions of varnish and linseed oil and turpentine are mixed. These rags can heat up spontaneously and cause fires. Safest practice is to rinse out rags in paint thinner and spread them out to dry outside on the ground. Dispose of all waste and dry rags in metal containers that permit air to enter. Antidotes for the toxic effects of drinking are listed on containers. Call a doctor at once if any of these materials are accidentally ingested by children. Good detergents are the cleaning agent for oil system materials.

Staining Wood

Of the several processes used to colour wood furniture without concealing the natural grain, staining is the most common and the simplest.

While it is acceptable and routine practice to tone wood shades and colours different from the natural colouring in the wood (toning walnut to look like mahogany, inferior woods to resemble birch, maple, walnut, etc.), the best looking furniture is that which is toned with colours that do not alter the basic character of the wood.

The general run of furniture woods can be classified colour-wise as belonging to a very few groups.

1. The brownish tones (walnut, brown mahogany).
2. Reddish tones (cherry, red mahogany).
3. Yellow tones (pine, birch, maple, poplar, oak, ash).
4. Orange tones (teak).

The yellow tone group (light woods which in their natural, raw-wood condition will appear to range from white through amber, tan and grey-green to yellow) are seldom finished completely natural. The finishes we call natural, or clear, actually involve some colouring in the wood—and these yellow tone woods are coloured towards brown, red, orange, amber or straw grey as desired.

The brown, red and orange woods, however, normally are toned only in their natural colour.

Any kind of wood can be toned with burnt umber (brown) and look well. Burnt umber, the basic wood colouring, is perfect for mahogany and walnut. To the other woods it gives a soft, aged look.

Yellow ochre, milked out with a little white will tone any of the yellow group to produce that 'natural wood' appearance.

The third most commonly used colour is burnt sienna (a reddish tone) that will give cherry its characteristic colour and produce a soft, red mahogany.

Burnt sienna and yellow ochre are the basic colours to produce an orange tone such as we use on teak, rock maple, pumpkin pine and the like.

All three of the basic colours can be mixed successfully and, in most cases, the orange tones do have a little burnt umber added to them.

You may take as a basic, general rule that any standard stain for the natural wood tones will be mixed with all three of the basic colours used in some proportion. (Cherry colour made from burnt sienna is all right, but add some burnt umber and a touch of yellow ochre and it looks better.)

The stain, itself, is made with oil pigments blended into a solvent which will soak into the wood and hold the colour in the wood when the finish is applied. Our basic solvent will be a mixture of paint thinner and boiled linseed oil.

Stains will not colour plastics, nor soak into finishes of any kind that are dry. They cannot be used as a finish like some one-step stain and finish materials on the market. They do not penetrate deeply in hardwood, but they are basic to furniture finishing and will be found in the best custom finish furniture. Many professionals use no other stains but these for their standard finishes.

You can purchase ready-made stains prepared with these same colours. However, such stains may not be usable for glazing or colour toning. The stains, pigments and formulas here are used for all-purpose colouring. Stick with them and be happy. Substitute ready-made stains for them and you may have reason to just sit down and bawl your eyes out.

The stains will be applied with brush and rag. They will require two to four hours to dry completely. They are inexpensive, safe to work with and match up with professional finishes because they are the basic colours of the trade. They are permanent colours that will not bleed, burn out, yellow or be affected by sunlight and other factors as many stains are. Like any colours, they react to ageing (which usually enhances their beauty) and to sunlight, but they are unexcelled in their permanence.

Burnt umber, burnt sienna and yellow ochre are the earth pigments used by the master painters of past centuries and today. Oil thinned out with paint thinner is the ideal solvent to colour wood.

The Materials and Tools

A two-inch bristle brush; a one-inch bristle brush; plain bristle scrubbing brush; artist's touch-up brush; some lint-free rags; tin cans; paint thinner (not turpentine); boiled linseed oil.

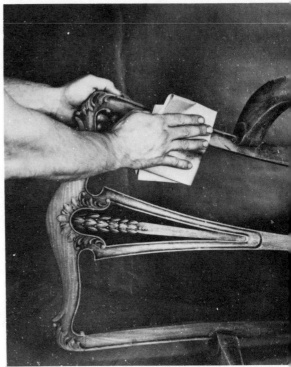

Red mahogany chair requires bleaching to take a light brown stain. Swab on any household bleach.

When the bleach has dried completely, sand down the wood with fine (F2 to 00) cabinet papers.

Colours can be painters' tinting oil colours, artists' oil colours, pigments ground in oil or the brand-named toning colours. Buy small quantities; the small can and the medium tube are fine. Get burnt umber, burnt sienna, yellow ochre, white, black, raw umber, chrome yellow (medium), Van Dyke brown and orange.

For experimental work have some scraps of walnut, pine, oak, mahogany, maple, etc.

For mixing, aluminium trays are unequalled. Aluminium foil in an old pie pan is fine.

The Stain Vehicle

Prepare the stain vehicle by mixing three parts of paint thinner with one part of boiled linseed oil. The proportion is not critical. Learn through experiments on different woods—and in accordance with the end results desired—to vary the amount of oil added to the thinner.

The oil hardens and gives body to the stain. It is something of a finish in itself. More oil produces a deeper, more lustrous colour, but too much oil will make the stain slow-drying and can result in gumminess if not wiped down with particular care. Experiment. On a piece of walnut or maple, apply some stain made with (1) paint thinner only (2) oil and thinner in the above proportions (3) oil and thinner mixed half and half and (4) oil without thinner. Use a little colour in it. Permit this to dry thoroughly and examine it to learn firsthand the difference in the mixtures so you can then use whatever proportions you want for a desired effect.

To see a stain as it will look finally, wet the

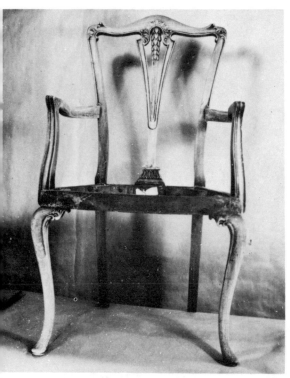

The mahogany is light enough to be toned brown with burnt umber after two bleach applications.

surface over the dried stain with a little oil or thinner.

Stains vary in their penetration of different woods. Softwood such as pine will drink up more stain and take on darker tones than is possible with walnut. Experiment by (1) using the standard proportion mix of oil and thinner (2) plain thinner (3) plain oil mixed about equally with pigment (burnt umber).

Apply these to pine, maple and walnut. Allow each to soak in thoroughly and then wipe it down and observe the contrast in the tone. You will see that the oil, which takes longer to soak in, will penetrate, carrying more colour with it than the thinner. You will also see that the softwood drinks up much more colour than the hard.

Observe also that the stain made with only thinner wipes off, carrying colour away, while the stain made with oil holds its colour better. When the oil is dry, the colour sticks; when the thinner is dry, a residue of colour can be wiped off. Therefore, our stains are made with enough oil to hold the colour when dry.

Mixing Colours

Blend the pigments before combining them with the vehicle. Use a little of the vehicle to permit a smooth blending. Test your colour on a scrap of wood like the wood of the piece of furniture you wish to stain to determine the shade, the intensity of penetration and the exact colour effect.

Experiment with combinations, applying them to a dark wood like walnut and a light wood like maple. In each case try the following mixtures in equal proportions, then alter them for comparison to acquaint yourself with the various tones possible:

1. Burnt umber and burnt sienna.
2. Burnt umber and yellow ochre.
3. Yellow ochre and burnt sienna.
4. Burnt umber, burnt sienna and yellow ochre.

When white is blended into one of these colours it milks it out. The colour changes slightly in tone as it is whitened. For example, milk down burnt umber until it is almost white and observe that it tends to grey out as it gets lighter.

We most often milk out the yellow tones for the lighter woods, so try the following colours on pine, maple, ash and oak. Combine the colours first in various proportions, and then milk them down by brushing or wiping white into the stain right on the wood.

1. Burnt umber.
2. Burnt sienna.
3. Yellow ochre.
4. Yellow ochre and burnt sienna.
5. Burnt sienna and burnt umber.
6. Burnt umber, yellow ochre and burnt sienna.

41

Filler makes a stain colour evenly. Note scratch which runs across the filled and unfilled areas.

Precoloured filler is applied to an open-grained wood with a brush or rag and left to haze over.

As you will see, yellow ochre and white milk down to a natural pine tone. Adding a small amount of burnt umber to it makes the tone even more true to 'natural' light wood. Combining small amounts of sienna and umber to the ochre and milking it down produces a soft, straw colour much like the oriental rice paper colours.

These light tones are what you will use to tone the light woods to a 'natural' look, running your colour towards the umber (brown), yellow (ochre), or red (sienna) as you wish. Walnut and mahogany are fine if toned simply with umber.

The other colours such as raw umber and chrome yellow are used for slight variations. The raw umber blended with white and burnt umber produces a greyish picking effect much used on pine. Raw umber can be used on oak also or on chestnut and hickory.

The chrome yellow is a truer colour than the ochre and is used particularly when blending the light tones to be milked down (in place of yellow ochre).

Black is used simply to darken the browns and to combine with red tones for special reddish brown effects.

Application of Stains to Wood

After you have tested your stain on scrap wood, then prepare a larger quantity for use. Ten or twelve ounces make enough stain for any average chest, table or sideboard. A teaspoon of pigment in a soup can of vehicle is about average for a medium-tone stain.

Brush or wipe the stain on with a rag. The brush permits you to lay it on heavier and permits more saturation. Let the stain soak in until you can see the change in its lustre as it penetrates and begins to dry. Then wipe it down thoroughly with a rag. Do not leave any residue on the surface. Check sides, panels and carvings to be sure the stain is not running.

Use a bristle brush to get into crevices, carvings and the like. Use a bristle scrubbing brush (dry) to burnish the stain into the wood, scrubbing with the grain. (When the stain has dried out completely, burnishing with the scrubbing

42

When the filler has begun to dry, it is rubbed off across the grain of the wood with a cloth.

brush will enhance the colour and surface appearance.)

If, after the piece is dry, you find any gummy spots where you did not wipe the stain down enough, use a little thinner on a rag to soften the gum and wipe it evenly.

A second application of stain may be necessary to produce an even tone of the colour or intensity you want. Apply it in the same way.

The more oil in the stain, the longer it can soak before drying and the harder it will dry. If you use an oily mixture, be particularly careful to wipe it down well to avoid hard, gum residue anywhere.

Applying the second coat with a mixture containing a little more oil than standard works well on hardwoods. Wipe this kind of application down well and burnish it with a cloth pad and scrubbing brush. One thin coat of finish over a perfectly burnished oily stain produces a beautifully finished product.

If you find that you have coloured the wood too dark, wipe it down with a rag wet with paint thinner at once and follow with a dry cloth.

If, after the stain is dry, it will not come off by scrubbing with a wet cloth as suggested above, then use a mixture of half paint thinner and half lacquer thinner. This will act like a very weak paint remover and cut off some of the colour.

In the unhappy event that you permit a very oily stain to dry heavily on the wood so it produces a skin or gumminess that will not wipe off by either of the above processes, then you must use paint remover (which you can weaken with half lacquer thinner) and scrub off the gum with steel wool.

Follow this with a good rubdown of just lacquer thinner which will dry out in an hour. Then you can restain at once.

Patch Colouring

Getting plastic wood and other repair material to take the same tone as the wood is the major problem in staining. Several other colouring processes will work to blend the patch in, as you will see, but in the staining itself, this is difficult.

Once again the importance of testing and keeping a control scrap with the work is evident. Before you apply a wood filler to spots, as you learned to do in the section on repair, mix and test your stain. Then colour the wood filler so that when it is dry, and stain is applied, it matches the rest of the wood.

For best results, use this procedure:

1. Make a flaw in the test piece and apply the wood filler which comes closest to the colour you get when you stain the wood. After it is dry and sanded smooth, stain the section and you will see that probably the patch is lighter than the stained wood.

2. Using the same oil colour you are making your stain from (save some colour when you make the stain), blend a very small amount into some of the wood filler to colour it. Then test this in the same way. After it is dry, sand it and apply stain over it and the wood. Does the patch blend in colour?

3. Touching up the patch with the stain colour after staining and before applying a finish will also be possible.

If filler is applied too heavily or permitted to dry until it is too hard, you'll require steel wool to scrub it off the wood.

After scrubbing off the filler, let it dry overnight. You may then wipe the surface clean, using a rag wet with paint thinner and adding colour if needed.

4. Wood patches or any wood with which you are going to repair the project should be of the same kind. Even so, it may not take the stain equally. So, before using any wood for repair, test it with the control sample to see how it does take the stain. You may have to darken it a little to match or you may have to use less colour. But know in advance. If the repair needs stronger colouring than the project wood, colour it separately before staining over the piece. If it requires less colour, mask it off when staining and touch it up separately afterwards—or experiment first! Apply a little boiled oil to the wood patch and let it soak in first so that when the stain is applied that part will not drink up so much stain.

But staining is only one way to colour and touch up wood. Colour toning, shading and glazing are all effective in achieving an equal tone over many kinds of woods and patches.

Colour Toning

When it is desirable to add more colour to the wood, over-all or in part, and staining will not do the job, the processes of colour toning, glazing and shading can be used.

Stains are thin dyes which soak into the wood, as you have seen. Colour toning,

44

Brushing stain on to a piece that did not require a filler. Let the stain soak in well and rub it down dry. Repeat this if needed.

shading, and glazing are techniques of applying colour on the wood rather than in it.

Colour toning is used mainly to balance up the contrasting colours or shades of parts of a piece of furniture which do not blend evenly with the rest. For example, a table top made of several four-inch-wide strips of maple takes the stain beautifully except that one strip down the centre is so light that the table top looks as though someone had painted a white streak over it. Rather than stain the entire top much darker, just to camouflage the one strip, we wipe colour on the light board to darken it.

Using the same pigment mixture that you made your stain from, blend the pigment with a very little oil-thinner vehicle to make a creamy paste. If necessary, mask off the errant strip on both sides. With a small cloth pad, wipe the colour on to the board. Use vehicle to thin it as necessary.

Rub the pigment until it does not wipe off with a dry rag. Burnish it into the wood as much as you can. A second or third application may be necessary, so do not try to get all the colour into the wood at one time. Do not lay a heavy, opaque 'paint' on the piece. The colour must be transparent to permit the grain of the wood to show through. It must be worked into

45

the wood throughly to avoid a painted look.

A dark section of wood can be lightened in the same way. Use the pigment from which you made your stain. Lighten it by adding some white, but do not milk the colour down too much. In many cases it will be best to lighten with ochre and white to avoid the milky tone.

Still another problem of colour balancing occurs when the colours rather than the shades of the woods vary—or when a piece of wood has a streak of irregular colour running through it. For example, adjoining pieces of mahogany on a chest top are yellowish and pinkish. You want to give a soft brown mahogany tone to the piece. After staining with a burnt umber stain, the pink cast of one piece and the yellow cast of the piece alongside it still show. To correct this, colour tone the pink area with ochre mixed with burnt umber (yellowish brown). Tone the yellow area with burnt sienna and burnt umber (reddish brown). Yellow and red combined to make orange, so now the two areas are closely matched in tone. You have altered them both to produce an orange-brown tone. To complete the balancing of colour, wipe burnt umber over the entire top.

A basic knowledge of colour mixing is necessary for the above type of colour toning and the following should be noted:

> Red and yellow become orange.
> Orange darkened becomes brown.
> Red and green become brown.
> Red and black become brown.

In nearly every case of colour toning where you must change the colour of a piece (rather than just its shade) it is best to work towards the basic wood colour, brown. This means that you want a brownish tone for the dark woods and a soft amber for the light woods. Therefore, the colour combinations that produce brown or its first cousin, orange, are all you need.

After equalizing the contrasting colours into a common, similar shade of brown or orange, go over the area with the colour you want for the entire piece.

There is just one way to learn all this: experiment.

1. A piece of mahogany has a black ink stain in it or any blackish flaw. Stain the piece with burnt umber. The black still shows miserably. Black and red make brown. Wipe burnt sienna into and on the black flaw.

The flaw may remain much too dark, even though now it has a brownish cast. Lighten it with a pigment mixture of burnt sienna and yellow ochre which will make an orange. Orange is a light brown. White is not necessary or desirable. Use the yellow ochre (which is light enough) to lighten the mixture.

When this is rubbed out thoroughly, it should make the spot lighter than the surrounding area of mahogany. The next step then is to darken it with burnt umber until it balances in tone.

If it is too pink, yellow it a little. If too yellow, red it a little. But finish off with the burnt umber.

2. A greenish streak runs through a piece of poplar or pine. You want a 'natural' straw tone to the wood.

Green and red make brown. Apply burnt sienna (red) to the streak until it kills the green tone and produces a brown tone. Now that will be much too dark for the finished product, but you have not finished.

Be sure the colour is dry so the next coating will not pick it up or wipe it off the green flaw. Then apply a mixture of yellow ochre and white (straw colour) to lighten the area. When this is dry, go over the piece with the original straw colour you want. In all cases when you colour tone over a large area, be sure you use a thin transparent colouring.

3. A piece of walnut requires toning to reduce contrasts much too strong for good appearance. After applying the proper tone to the contrasting areas, blend the colours together with your cloth pad so that you 'feather' them into each other, leaving no harsh line of separation.

Glazing

Glazing is the process of applying a very thin, transparent tint of colour to the surface of

46

the wood or over a coat of clear finish such as varnish or lacquer sealer before applying the final finish coats.

As applicable to clear finishes, glazing is used mostly on maple, birch and pine for very subtle alterations of colour and tone. Glazes are used also to slightly haze over wood filled with minor flaws and produce a very even toning.

Glazes give plain woods like clear pine or maple a little character by way of adding some very fine brushed on lines to imitate grain. Those which are going to have a finish sprayed over them can be made of paint thinner, pigment and a few drops of oil. The only reason for the oil is to slow down the drying time enough to permit easy working, because paint thinner with so very little pigment in it will dry in minutes and not permit careful work. Glazes over which you are going to brush or wipe a finish must be made like stain so they will have enough oil in them to dry out and stick.

Prepare your colour more thinly than a stain. Brush it on the raw or finished surface with fast, careful strokes, wiping your brush dry constantly and stroking in the direction of the grain of the wood. As the glaze gets tacky, the brush strokes will leave fine lines. If you want to apply a completely unlined, transparent tone, you must brush it out very fast. Work only one area on a piece at a time.

Experiment and with a little practice you can learn to handle a glaze made with varnish and paint thinner rather than oil and paint thinner. Prepare the glaze by mixing one part of varnish with three to five parts of paint thinner and adding colour. Try this on a piece of wood that has been given one coat of finish of any kind and is free of wax and grease.

To determine if your mixture is correct, wait until the glaze has dried about three hours and then coat it with varnish, brushing hard to see if the glaze sticks or is picked up. If the glaze does not stick, you need more varnish in the mixture. If you find that the glaze is drying too fast for you to brush it out smoothly, add some boiled linseed oil to it.

Experiment with imitating grain. Use a piece of clear light wood. Prepare a glaze with the colour made of burnt umber and burnt sienna, being sure this glaze is heavy enough with colour so that you brush some clearly visible dark lines on the wood.

Using the oil-paint thinner (no varnish) with the colour for your glaze, brush it over the wood. With a clean, dry brush (a three-inch brush is excellent) made of soft hair, stroke the glaze the long way of the board with the grain. As the glaze gets tacky enough to hold the colour despite your brushing, stroke across the board and across the strokes you made first. You will see that this produces a pattern that closely resembles the grain of wood.

Graining is a fine art. Few finishers can grain very well, so do not feel self-conscious if your work is not perfect. But this little graining trick can be used to fine advantage to camouflage repair spots and small sections of clear wood that need some character (sofa legs, for example).

Shading

Shading is done mostly with spray equipment. The process consists only of spraying a thin transparent coating of colour on wood to conceal flaws, balance the tone of irregular woods or achieve certain finished tones easier than through staining or glazing. It is also used for artistic effects to darken carved areas and the like.

Shading without a gun is done like colour toning. Over the first coat of finish wipe colour into carvings or trim or on legs to provide a subtle highlight-shade effect. Use a vehicle made of varnish and paint thinner so it will stick well to the finish. You can apply the shading with cloth or with brush.

Adding colour to a finish coat of varnish to be brushed on is, in effect, shading the piece. As you see, shading and glazing, when used to apply a transparent tone, are much the same.

Filling Wood

Permit the filler to partially dry on the surface. It dulls out as it is drying. Do not permit

You can accent mouldings or carvings by brushing dark colour such as burnt umber into depressions.

Blotches, stains or other ugly discoloured areas can sometimes be concealed by colour toning.

Wipe off the surplus colour on mouldings or carvings carefully so that highlights add contrast.

it to dry completely or you will not be able to wipe it off. When the filler has taken on a dull lustre, wipe it down thoroughly with a coarse rag such as burlap. Wipe across the grain to get the heavy filler away from the wood while leaving it in the grain pores. Finish wiping with the grain until all the surplus filler is removed from the surface of the wood. If necessary, use a piece of rag wetted with paint thinner.

When the piece has dried for four to eight hours, check it to see if any spots of dried filler remain on the surface. These must be removed either with a paint thinner, scrubbing rag, steel wool or by sanding with fine papers ($1\frac{1}{2}$, 00). Stain over the piece if you had to sand it or if you wish to add more colour. Then proceed with the regular finishing such as colour toning, glazing, shading and the final finish.

Do not fill wood that is to receive a flat oil or oil-resin finish.

Note: the light grain spots that show up on many types of furniture after a few years are due to the filler changing colour faster than the wood. This is particularly common on the commercial finishes known mainly as blonde oak or blonde mahogany.

You will see that open-grain finishes on walnut and mahogany as well as oak are quite handsome, except in the high gloss finishes.

In passing, let us note that filler can be applied over a coat of sealer or in other ways for special purposes; however, these are primarily professional devices and you will have little if any use for the methods. It is used mostly on raw wood to help prepare a smooth surface for a clear finish.

Removing Filler

Pieces that you are refinishing may be loaded with filler. The paint remover and the methods normally used do not always get out all the old filler from the mahogany or walnut. Use a wire brush and scrub lightly with the grain. This brushing is also used on any grainy wood to acquire an open-grain texture or, as you will see, when making certain decorator finishes.

The only purpose for filling porous wood is to fill the grain pores so that you can produce a finished surface that is without the open-grain look. This applies almost entirely to walnut, mahogany and oak.

Ready-made fillers are available at paint and finish suppliers. Use a paste filler that is precoloured in one of the basic wood tones such as walnut, mahogany or maple.

Filler can be applied before or after staining. Coloured filler acts as stain and filler combined, but if you have to sand the piece afterwards to cut off residue filler, it will be necessary to restain the piece.

Apply the filler with an old brush. Be sure it is liquid enough to handle easily, and thin it with paint thinner as necessary. Some fillers cannot be thinned with paint thinner. Check when you buy.

The Clear Finishes

It can be stated generally that all finishes are made of resins, solvent and drying agents. The methods for handling the very few basically different finishes depend mainly upon the type of solvent which is necessary in the manufacture of the finish.

Lacquer is soluble in a specially formulated solvent known, logically enough, as lacquer thinner. Varnish is soluble in linseed oil, certain other oils and a group of solvents called paint thinners. Lacquer and varnish do not mix. Their solvents cannot be used interchangeably.

Shellac is soluble in alcohol and methylated spirit. It generally is not mixed with varnish and never with lacquer.

It is best to refer to the materials used in any type of finishing process in groups such as the oil system, the lacquer system and the shellac system. By these terms we mean not only the basic type of finish but the solvents used, the colouring materials and all other materials and methods that apply strictly to each system.

Now, to begin with, let's set the record straight about finishes and which are and are not the best. A good deal of mythology has sprung up under the nourishment of so-called 'experts'. They have written all too many books and articles asserting boldly and dogmatically that linseed oil or French polish or some exotic currently unknown material or mixture was the

50

There is no more beautiful finish than oil-resin for a classic tilt-top table such as the one shown.

Oil-resin is shown here being applied to a teak table. It can be spread with a rag or bare hands.

Use steel wool to rub down the oil-resin for the smoothest possible finish before the final coat.

Burnish oil-resin with a pad, as shown, to make it as dry and smooth as hand rubbing can make it.

'secret' of the master finishers of past centuries. These same uninformed characters have maligned varnish, claiming that it was never used on 'antiques', should not be used and is no good.

Nothing could be further from the truth nor more specifically point up how fantastic a 'system' of erroneous ideas can be created by completely uninformed people in a field where few men have taken the time for standard research, depending rather on old wives' tales, guesses and their own practice as rank amateurs. Few finishers or 'experts' on antiques know the first thing about the chemistry of

51

finishes. Nor do they bother researching to actually determine facts before they write their myths.

Varnish, so maligned, was the finish used by the masters as far back as the time of the Pharaohs in Egypt. Varnish made of oils and resins was applied with leather pads, cloths or bare hands to produce the very finishes that we so admire today and usually try to copy with everything conceivable except varnish.

Like so many 'tricks' of master artisans in any field, the resin-oil (varnish) finish is probably the least tricky, but it is not applied in the manner a painter would put it on a floor. Nor is it ever applied to furniture according to the directions on varnish cans. Quite the opposite as we shall see.

The Classic Oil-resin Finish

The formula for a good oil-resin varnish is as follows: Two (2) parts synthetic fast-dry quality varnish (alkyd type) to supply the basic resin and drier; one (1) part boiled linseed oil; and three (3) parts quality paint thinner.

This mixture approximates classic formulas and works equally well if not better because of the characteristics of the modern resins. Prepare it several days before you intend to use it and put it in a sealed container in a cool and moderately dry place.

The oil-resin can be worked into the wood with a brush, a rag or your bare hands. Let it soak in and, as it does, apply more to spots that are drinking it up until the wood will take no more. Do not let the surface dry out. Give the wood time to soak up but keep an eye on it. Ordinarily, after about an hour the wood will have taken enough of the solution. Then wipe down the surface well. If there is any tackiness at all, cut it with paint thinner and wipe it out until it is tack-free.

Permit this first application to dry out overnight at least and then apply another treatment of the oil-resin if needed.

Before applying a second or third coat, check the surface to see if any of the wood is unsaturated. If the oil-resin has penetrated evenly over-all, the appearance of the surface

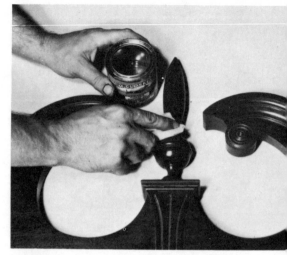

Wipe flattening oil carefully into all surfaces of the wood for a truly classic antique patina.

Wipe on stain. When it has dried (2 to 6 hours, depending on mixture) apply varnish to surface.

will be quite even. If it has not, the spot that needs more treatment will show.

After the first or second coat has dried overnight, and you see that another treatment is not

52

Study these three photos and then practise the motion in dry run to perfect brushing technique.

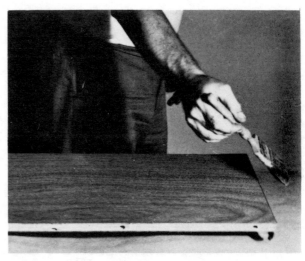

Start the brush stroke on the board as shown and then swing it completely off the end—and up . . .

required to saturate the wood, apply a finish dressing using the same mixture of oil-resin. However, this finish coat must be rubbed down at once until it is 'dry' and tack-free so that it will collect no dust. Very much as you would wax a surface and burnish it, apply the oil-resin with a small cloth pad and rub it down with a leather or flannel pad. Use a little lubricant if necessary to permit smooth rubbing. Make the lubricant from a mixture of one part boiled linseed oil and one part paint thinner.

Real hand rubbing of a finish is the process of polishing in this manner or with the palm of your hand. There is no finer tool for the purpose. A pair of leather gloves slightly wet with the lubricating mixture permits you to use your hands and fingers to do a magnificent job of rubbing down the finish. And when this finish is dry, it requires no further rubbing or polishing at all. It is largely in the wood, not on top of it. It will not peel or crack or chip as a varnish coating that has been heavily flowed on top of the wood.

On your return stroke—and this is of the utmost importance—hit the board INSIDE the edge.

53

Jam your brush into corners to get a good but rather dry application of the varnish, as above.

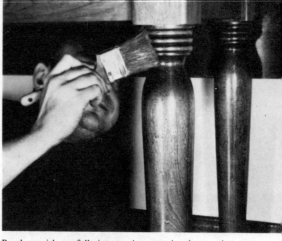

Brush varnish carefully into turnings, treating them as tiny corners, and use an almost dry brush.

The foregoing process of application eliminates drips, runs, overlaps and dust collection. The finish is substantial, being much harder and protective than an 'oil' finish. Also, as you will see, it is unequalled in beauty. And yet, what could be simpler to apply?

The so-called 'oil finish' much touted by those 'experts' was a resin-oil mixture unless the finisher could not obtain resin. Then he was forced to settle for the linseed oil alone, which in its raw form took months to dry and required coat after coat to saturate the wood enough to produce a solid finish.

Flat Oil Finish

The modern dead flat oil finish made popular with Danish furniture is most easily achieved with flattening oil, a specially formulated oil sold under names like Danish oil or teak oil. Thinned out with paint thinner (2 parts oil, 1 part thinner), it can be applied like the oil-resin finish or simply brushed on. It is allowed to soak in and then wiped down well. A little varnish can be added to it to give it body. This is especially applicable to table tops for greater protection.

Do not apply flattening oil over other finishes of any kind. It is formulated to be applied to unfinished wood only.

On most pieces, the oil-resin finish will be dull enough (if rubbed with steel wool after it is dry) to serve as a flat oil finish. You can vary the proportions of the oil-resin formula for this purpose. By using less oil and a greater proportion of thinner to produce a rather thin mix and then applying only one coat and touching that up only where dry spots need it, you can get a finish very close to the flat oil type.

Colouring Oil and Oil-resin Finishes

Because oil pigments will mix perfectly with the flat oil or oil-resin, you can colour the wood as you apply a coat of finish and rub it down. This should be done to the first or second coat, never to the final coat. Always finish clear over any colouring.

While the finish is still 'wet' wipe colour into it wherever you wish to alter the tone or shade. Prepare your pigment simply by adding colour to a small amount of the finish liquid.

In between coats you can touch up spots with an artist's brush, using the same pigments

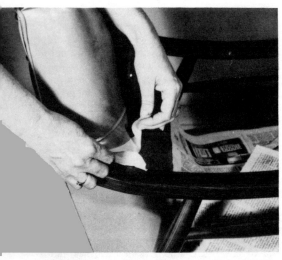

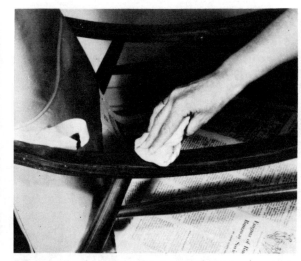

Mask off a leather chair to protect areas before dressing wood with varnish or oil-resin finish.

One application of varnish wiped on walnut will impart a fine, soft look to the grain of the wood.

and mixture. Do this after you have wiped the piece down. Apply the touch-up colour thin so as not to build up ridges. A delicate line here and there on repair spots may make considerable difference in the final appearance of the piece.

Varnish

Varnish can be applied to the raw wood or over another finish if you brush it on. Do not apply it directly from the original can. Thin your varnish with paint thinner, using at least two parts of thinner to one part varnish.

Do not flow the mixture on. It will run, drip, ridge and collect dust. Brush it into the wood thoroughly and evenly, leaving no wet pools of varnish on the surface. Work with semi-dry brush at all times to do this.

Apply the finish to difficult spots first, leaving the nice flat surfaces until last. Get into the corners of panel sections and get at the little raised edges, the carvings, the turnings and all difficult spots before you apply the varnish to the adjoining flat areas. Brush these spots out thoroughly.

Use a back-and-forth slapping motion of the brush to do round legs. Jam the brush up into openings and filigree—and look carefully for runs over these hard-to-get-into spots. Brush out the runs and drips at once. If you forget or miss some, and the varnish is not completely dry, wipe down the excess with paint thinner. If it is dry, then you can cut it away from the edge or sand it down level.

Application of varnish by brush will generally leave the surface not quite perfect. Some light sanding will usually be necessary to cut off dust flecks and get a smooth surface for the next coat.

You may find that one thin coat of varnish will do nicely on woods like walnut or mahogany. Perhaps all you will have to do is rub the finish down with 4-0 steel wool and burnish it with a dry, soft cloth.

You must use your own judgment as to the finished effect you are after. One thin coat of varnish burnished into the wood is very much like the oil-resin finish and does work nicely for many pieces, particularly the frames of Victorian sofas and chairs and the like. Table tops and tops of chests usually need a second or third coat for greater protection. These fol-

55

A transparent glaze will alter the tone of the clear finish slightly. Mask off surrounding areas.

down with even finer papers or rubbed in various ways to achieve the desired lustre.

Flat, eggshell and semi-gloss varnishes are available. Even the dull flat type is alcohol-proof. You cannot rub down a flat varnish without raising lustre higher. When you apply a final coat of a varnish that you are not going to rub down, be particularly careful to avoid dust. Brush the varnish on smoothly and evenly and do not try to work it in as you did the first coat. For this final unrubbed coat, a mixture of half varnish and half paint thinner can be used. Too thin a mixture will not go on evenly and will result in a patchy dull and gloss finish.

If necessary, avoid settlement of dust on the tops of chests or tables by setting the piece with the top vertical. After applying the varnish, let it remain in that position until it sets up enough not to hold dust. Alkyd resin varnishes, like similar-type varnishes, will set up dust-free in as little as five minutes in a warm, well-ventilated place when the varnish has been thinned down.

While it is impractical to attempt colour toning when applying varnish with a brush, thin glazes can be applied to a dry coat if the glaze is made with a little varnish to make it stick well. A thin mixture of varnish and colour can be used for colour toning over a dry area. But this is too difficult to attempt on large surfaces such as table tops. Use it only for small touch-up on arms, legs and the like. When you intend to brush on a varnish finish, be sure your colouring is right first.

Lacquer

Lacquer has generally replaced varnish as a finish in the furniture manufacturing field as well as in custom finishing. However, because it requires spray equipment and special facilities (booth and exhaust system) the lacquer system of finishing has not been made generally available to the home craftsman.

Small spray guns and compressors are proving capable of handling most of the work a hobbyist would do, but to acquire a semi-professional-type and compressor that is dependable and generally usable is much more expensive. Other spraying gizmos such as the

lowing coats are applied just like the original, but first examine the dried surface of the piece to see if it needs sanding. If so, use one of the wet-type finishing papers made especially for sanding down finish coats. The grades are marked in hundreds. A No. 400 paper will cut off most varnish flaws without doing damage. Use the paper with a little water as a lubricant.

Varnish can be applied in thin coats like this and sanded carefully in between each application until you have built up a smooth, glass-like surface. The final coat is then sanded

56

Be very careful you do not damage the edges of a piece when fine-sanding surface of finish coat.

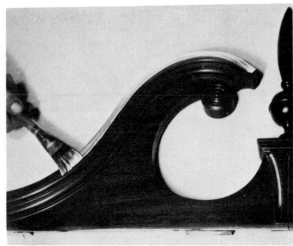

If a trim is desired, apply the gold or silver before the application of final coat of varnish.

When dry, varnish is wet-sanded (with water) using fine No. 400 paper—then with No. 600 for gloss.

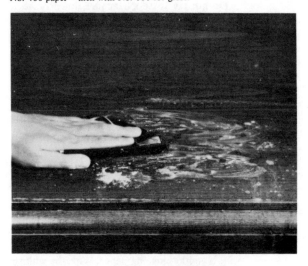

electric type or the attachments for vacuum cleaners are hardly worth discussing.

The aerosol pressure can is usable for some work with lacquer, but until the people who sell these cans have designed a spray tip that is completely dependable, you have a booby trap that may suddenly go berserk. Nevertheless, the aerosol can is here to stay and it is the lacquer applicator most generally available to the hobbyist. It offers the advantage of containing ready-mixed lacquers, sealers and shaders —and when it goes wrong, it is a satisfying size for hurling under full muscle power as far as possible.

The pressure in an aerosol can will squirt globs and heavy drops at irregular intervals. You cannot outguess it apparently, but you can outwit it most of the time. Be sure your finger tip does not go beyond the plastic spray tip. Keep your finger well back on that tip. To fully appreciate why, go ahead and put your finger out over the tip and watch the lacquer splash against your finger, flinging great globs of lacquer over any surface you are spraying.

When you buy a can of lacquer, try out the tip at the store to be sure you can spray a fine mist with it evenly. Before spraying any piece of furniture, try the can on some scrap to see if you have a reasonable chance of succeeding, or if you have acquired a troublesome, uncooperative renegade.

57

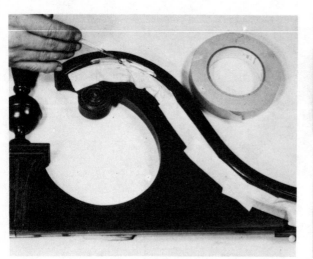

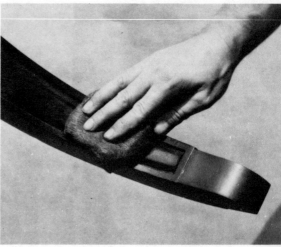

Play safe and use masking tape for protection if painting trim on carved or recessed areas, above.

Use 4-0 steel wool—gently—to soften gloss of final coat of brushed or hand-rubbed varnish.

Do not try to shoot lacquer down on to a surface as you do when using a gun. By tipping the furniture so you can shoot straight out at the surface, you have a fighting chance to avoid splatter. Work with the can as far away from the piece as is reasonable. The farther away, the less chance of splatter.

If globs of lacquer do splatter on a surface, stop shooting at once. Let the lacquer dry for about a half hour. Using a fine cabinet paper (Tri-M-Ite No. 320 or No. 400) carefully sand the surface with particular attention to the heavy splatter spots. Sand until the spots are levelled out with the rest of the surface. Then you can continue spraying.

To finish a piece with lacquer over stain and colour toning, first spray on a very light coat of lacquer sanding sealer. Allow this to dry one half hour or more. Carefully sand the sealer with No. 400 finishing paper. Wipe the whitish sealer dust off with a rag sparsely wet with paint thinner. (Lacquer thinner will dissolve the sealer and ruin the work.) The paint thinner will dry off very fast and then you can spray over the smooth, sanded sealer with lacquer.

Apply a moderately thin coat, allowing it to dry for one or two hours. Once again, sand with No. 400 paper. Then clean with a paint thinner tack rag and apply another coat.

In similar manner, you can build several coats of lacquer to acquire the appearance you want in the finish. The final coat of lacquer should be sanded with No. 400 if it is gritty. Then sand with No. 600 if you want a glossy surface. Follow up with 4-0 steel wool and/or rubbing compound.

Lacquers are available in various degrees of lustre. Purchase what you need from dead flat to high gloss to use for the final, finish dress coat. If you apply the final coat very carefully, you will not have to sand it or rub it down.

Shading lacquer is also available in pressure cans. You can obtain mahogany, walnut and the like. Use this shader to subtly alter the tone achieved in staining if you need it. Apply sealer over the shader and proceed as before to complete the finish. Do not sand the shading coat or it will not be evenly distributed over the piece.

Often, a combination of lacquer applied with the pressure can and varnish or oil-resin work

The photos here and on the next page show removal of residue after applying a rubbing compound.

Sanding drawers to make them ride better.

well. Using the varnish or oil-resin on the top of a cabinet or table, you then can use the pressure can of lacquer for the legs or sides.

Varnish can be applied over lacquer. Do not spray lacquer over varnish or oil-resin. The lacquer will act almost like a paint remover on the varnish. Thus you can shade a piece with lacquer shader from a can, you can seal it with sanding sealer and then you can apply a finish of brushed varnish.

Lacquer sealer is also very useful when you colour tone or touch up. In place of using a vehicle for the colour that has oil in it to make it stick, you can use just paint thinner with colour. This dries very fast. Then shoot a light coat of clear lacquer sanding sealer over it to bind it. Immediately, you can tone over the sealer, glaze over it or continue with the finish varnish.

Use of Spray Equipment

This book is not intended for the hobbyist using professional lacquering methods. However, a word of advice: When you work with lacquer, use the material well thinned out with lacquer thinner. It is much better to apply several coats of thin lacquer than one heavy, hard-to-work, hard-to-apply coat. Clean your gun before and after using by spraying lacquer thinner through it. Loosen the pot after use to prevent it from sticking.

Brand-named colours (not oil colours) can be used to tint lacquer. Do not use regular oil stains or heavy oil glazes. Use paint thinner as your vehicle. Add very little oil if needed for slower working time.

Do not try to apply lacquer over any other finish except lacquer and lacquer sealer.

The finest lacquers are those made for the automotive trade. These are generally superior to industrial lacquers used on furniture.

If you spray, do so outside. Do not use any common fans to blow the fine lacquer dust and gases away. One electrical spark can cause a fatal explosion. Special exhaust fans are made to be used for this purpose. Never spray in a building where there is so much as a pilot light lit on a stove.

Lacquer vapours are not designed for human consumption, and they are highly explosive.

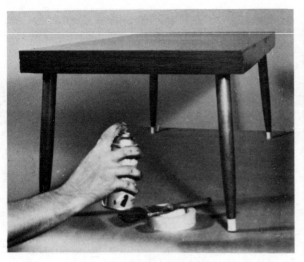

Spraying table legs after masking brass tips.

Spraying work in an upright position to avoid spattering gobs of lacquer.

Keep finger back from spray!

Professionals do not wear any metal when working with lacquer. Brass is used on exhaust equipment to eliminate sparks. The best advice to the home hobbyist: Do not use lacquer spraying equipment anywhere inside any building.

Shellac

Shellac can be used on small wooden items. Thin it out with four to five parts of alcohol or 'shellac thinner' or methylated spirit. Brush on small areas at a time, working fast in smooth, light strokes. Overlap each stroke as you go along. Do not try to go over it. Shellac sets up much too fast to permit any real brushing.

To smooth out a shellacked surface, you can sand lightly with No. 400 paper. You can also use a little methylated spirit and a brush to go back over the surface very lightly.

Apply several coats of thin shellac. Allow each coat to dry out two to four hours before sanding.

Shellac offers no particular advantage as a finish. There are few if any cases where varnish or oil-resin are not better.

Shellac will not darken a light, clear wood like varnish or oil will, however. If you wish to preserve any such wood as light as possible, use shellac first or throughout as a finish. Varnish can be applied over shellac.

60

Controlling Degree of Gloss

It is easy to get a high gloss finish and more difficult to keep a finish soft and lustrous. Rubbing the finish with 4-0 steel wool to an even lustre and then rubbing down with a flannel or chamois pad will give a high sheen that is not garish like unrubbed plain gloss varnish, shellac or lacquer. Application of wax over this increases the shine.

For a satin finish, use a flat varnish. When this is rubbed down with 4-0 steel wool it leaves a soft lustre. Still flatter finishes are produced when you eliminate the rubbing and simply brush on a very thin final coat of flat or eggshell varnish.

As mentioned before, the dead flat 'oil finish' is created by application of flat oil which dries overnight.

You can use 3-0 steel wool, a little coarser than 4-0, for rubbing, but on flat surfaces you must rub evenly the full length of the piece so that all the fine lines cut by the wool are parallel with the grain. Rub until all the gloss of the finish is removed and the surface texture is smooth and even.

The fine lines cut into the finish by any steel wool or compound are what cut the gloss. They produce tiny grooves that break up the light reflection very much like frosted glass or other glass finished in a way to leave such grooves. Gloss results from a smooth, glass-like surface. Reduction of gloss comes from cutting that surface with fine lines or through addition to the finish of a flattening agent (the whitish stuff in flat varnish which will absorb light rather than reflect it).

Rubbing can make the surface dull by leaving fine lines. Finer and finer rubbing materials will level off the surface until it is glass-like and achieve the highest possible gloss (just as polishing glass with fine powder does).

Steel wool or coarse rubbing compound will cut the gloss. Pumice, rottenstone and fine rubbing compound will increase the gloss while removing the harsh glare of varnish, shellac, lacquer or enamel.

If your finish coat is pitted or has drips or other irregularities in it, then it is a waste of time to begin rubbing with steel wool. Use Wet-or-Dry paper, beginning with grade No. 400 or No. 320 for coarser work. This is a special paper designed to be used on finishes. It is extremely fine and even. Use water as a lubricant and 'sand' the surface carefully, working always with the grain. Do not use much pressure. The wet sanding will produce a fine paste which will have to be wiped off before adding another thin coat of finish or giving it a final rubbing with the steel wool.

After using the No. 400 grade paper, use of No. 600 grade in itself will produce a fine rubbed finish similar to that achieved with 3-0 steel wool.

Using Steel Wool

On flat top surfaces where the rubbing must be even and regular to look right, use a flat cloth pad on top of the wool and back this up with a perfectly flat piece of wood like a sanding block. If you buy the steel wool in a continuous ribbon rather than in pads, make a pad by smoothly wrapping the wool into a flat bundle of three or four thicknesses.

Keep your arm moving straight. No circles. Move over the entire length of the top (as when sanding). Do not apply pressure at the edge or you will cut through the finish into the wood.

Steady, regular rubbing will eliminate all the gloss and produce a fine lustrous surface with all rubbing lines parallel and even. Never rub across the grain. To find out why, experiment on a sample. One pass across the grain and you will spend the next two weeks rubbing with the grain to eliminate those crosscuts.

If you do goof and get crosscuts, then you should go back to the No. 400 or No. 600 paper to eliminate them before proceeding to proper rubbing with the grain. It takes willpower and practice to rub straight and not make a big arc, as is the natural path of the arm swinging from the shoulder.

Do the ends first. Rub carefully in short strokes with the grain to get the end rubbed down. Then go over the whole top and take it easy on those ends. Rub round legs around, not with the grain.

Keeping finger well back from spray tip prevents splattering and messing of both work and fingers.

Spraying too close to the work causes lacquer to build up and, though fast-drying, it will run.

SANDING lightly with No. 400 paper between varnish coats (being careful not to cut through) will improve your final finish by eliminating irregularities as you build the finish.

If the rubbing paste (resulting from using the paper wet) is hard to get out of small depressions, use a scrubbing brush.

Standard Clear Finishes

Following are step-by-step procedures for staining, colour toning and finishing different woods after the piece has been stripped, repaired and sanded for the finish:

American Cherry

New wood. (Hard, light in colour and often almost as light as birch.)

Stain: Burnt umber and burnt sienna, half and half in a vehicle (oil-thinner). Colour tone with the same mix if necessary.

Finish: Brushed varnish. Two or three coats. Sand with No. 400 between coats. Sand final coat with No. 400. Rub with 4-0 steel wool.

Old wood. (Much softer and darker in colour. Smells sweet and powders finely when sanded.)

Stain: Only if necessary. Then use just a tint of the same as for new wood and apply it thin.

Finish: Oil-resin burnished into wood, two to three applications.

Maple and Birch

Stain: For an amber tone, use burnt sienna and yellow ochre mixed as desired for the exact tone; for a brown tone, use burnt umber; for a

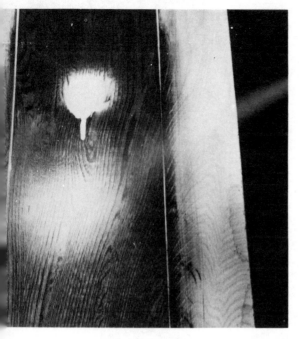

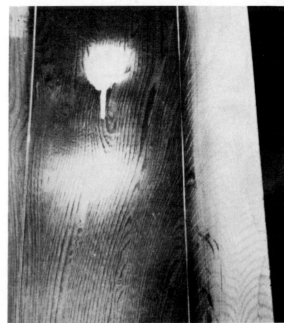

Above left: This photo shows that a shot of lacquer will go on properly at distance of about 10 to 12 inches.

Above right: The other extreme is shown above. Holding can too far from work does not permit good coverage.

Right: Same rules apply to spray gun. Hold it like a pistol and use spray like an invisible brush.

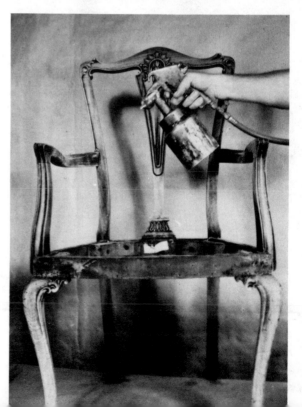

reddish (rock maple) tone, use burnt sienna and a little burnt umber; for a light, natural tone, mix yellow ochre and white half-and-half and add a touch of burnt sienna.

Finish: Brushed varnish, sanded between coats with No. 400. Finish coat sanded with No. 400 and rubbed with 4-0 steel wool. One coat will do for most cases.

Lacquer may be used in place of varnish. If so, apply one coat sanding sealer. Sand with No. 400. Apply one coat of semigloss or flat lacquer. Sand with No. 400 if necessary. Rub lightly with 4-0 steel wool.

Novelist's wife, Mrs. Will Saxon, writes at fine old desk restored in soft brown mahogany finish.

Mrs. Saxon displays another refinished piece and points out fact that old brass was also restored.

Early American dough box end table was finished with clear oil-resin and wet-sanded to high gloss. Matching tones of new and old pieces is trick here.

Walnut

Stain: Burnt umber.

Finish: One or two coats of flattening oil or an oil-resin burnished coating (one coat).

If there are light, sappy streaks in the wood, colour tone carefully with burnt umber.

A quick one-coat finish can be used. Add burnt umber colour to the flattening oil or oil-resin mixture.

If lacquer is used, apply one coat of sealer and one coat of dead flat lacquer. Do not sand or rub down the lacquer finish in this case.

Victorian Walnut

Stain: Burnt umber. Colour tone as necessary for an even walnut shade.

Finish: Oil-resin. Use two to three applications well burnished into the wood.

For a perfectly smooth, closed-grain table top surface, fill the wood first with walnut filler. Apply two to three coats of brushed varnish over the filler. Sand with No. 400 between coats. Finish final coat with flat varnish applied very thin. If gritty after dry, rub lightly with 4-0 steel wool.

Mahogany

Stain: For a red mahogany, use burnt sienna; for a brown mahogany, use burnt umber. Varying shades made by combining burnt umber and burnt sienna also work well. Fill the grain if a closed-grain surface is desired.

Finish: Brush varnish on a filled surface, sanding between coats with No. 400 paper. Finish coat flat or gloss as desired.

Oil-resin finish can be used on open-grain (unfilled) wood.

For lacquer, first apply one coat of sanding sealer. Shade if desired with red or brown mahogany shader. Apply two to three coats of lacquer, flat or gloss as desired. Sand with No. 400 between coats. Finish final coat to gloss desired (rubbing and sanding as needed).

Pickled Pine

Stain: None or a natural tone made of yellow ochre and burnt umber, milked down with white.

Glaze: Raw umber and burnt umber, half-and-half. Milk down with white to get a grey cobweb colour. Add a little ochre if desired for less greyish cast.

Glaze with brush, applying thin. When thoroughly dry, coat with one application of lacquer sealer or brush on carefully a very thin coat of varnish. (Not more than one part varnish to four parts thinner.) When dry, apply lacquer or brushed varnish over the lacquer sealer. If thinned varnish was used to seal, apply brushed varnish as finish coat. Rub finish with 4-0 steel wool.

Oak

Stain: Burnt umber for a brown medieval finish; burnt umber and raw umber, half-and-half for a renaissance finish; yellow ochre with a little burnt umber for normal brown oak.

Finish: Brushed varnish, sanded and rubbed. Lacquer can be used.

Glazes work well on oak because of the heavy grain. After staining, seal with thin varnish or lacquer sealer. Wipe a darker tone into the grain. Burnt umber works well. Raw umber will give the piece an interesting pickled effect.

Modern living allows the combination of new and unusual pieces—provided clear lines and wood tones are either related or refinished to match. *[Fine Hardwood Association Photo.]*

The Painted Finishes

PAINTED finishes include both the opaque coatings designed to completely conceal the colour and grain of wood (standard paints, enamels and lacquer enamels) and semi-opaque coatings designed to utilize part of the grain or natural colour of the wood to produce finished effects quite interesting, however unnatural they are. (These include the palomino or two-tone finishes and the wash coat and glaze finishes.)

Many contemporary pieces of commercial furniture which appear to be finished with clear coatings, where it seems the grain of the wood is clearly evident, are in fact covered with painted finishes. Common examples include most blonde mahoganies, blonde and a host of other light oak finishes, French walnut, fruitwood and the many shades and types of light brown mahogany and walnut.

Semi-opaque finishes provide many of our most interesting finishes. Wash coat and glaze finishes also are good looking. But the primary reason for the wash or glaze coat is to inexpensively achieve finishes otherwise commercially impractical.

French walnut is an excellent example. It is a handsomely-grained, light-toned wood much in favour in America. However, the 'French walnut' furniture commonly sold is made of dark American walnut, with much of the grain of the wood sacrificed to produce a finish that only approximates the true French walnut.

A semi-transparent wash coat in a light, neutral wood tone is sprayed over the piece to colour balance unmatched pieces of wood and conceal all kinds of flaws and patching. The wash coat does not fill the grain of the walnut. A light walnut glaze (or shader) is then applied over the wash coat. This, of course, gets into the open grain of the wood and tones the whole piece to a French walnut colour. However, the grain of the wood is revealed only in part. Presto! French walnut.

But we will explain the process in detail later. Let's get on with some basic terms that we shall use in discussing painted finishes:

Paint: Interior fast-drying types, both the oil-base paints which are thinned with paint

This handsome frame of 'Boy With Book', a pastel by Ray Boynton, was accomplished with gesso, texturing and gold glazing.

Simple but attractive, the finish on this chest is a combination of 'gesso' and transparencies.

67

thinner and the synthetic paints such as latex and vinyl which can be thinned with water. We also include the other water-soluble paints such as calcimine.

Exterior paints such as are normally used for houses can be used on furniture but, because of slowness in drying and other characteristics, it is best to stay away from these and stick with the interior paints.

Enamel: Never use inferior, cheap enamel. Enamel is basically varnish to which has been added a colour pigment. Interior enamels should be used on furniture. Select a fast-drying type from among the several reputable brands on the market. Enamels are oil base and are compatible with the oil system materials such as varnish, oil colours and other oil-base paints.

Lacquer enamel: Lacquer which has been coloured with pigment is called lacquer enamel. Ordinarily applied with spray equipment. Also available in aerosol cans for limited use. Compatible only with the lacquer system.

Ghesso: A heavy-bodied, paste-like opaque paint which can be used to provide a smooth surface over crude and unfinished materials, including wood, cloth and paper. Used for decorative effects when textured and/or glazed. We will make our own ghesso from water-soluble interior flat paint. The paste that results from leaving some types of this paint open to the air makes a fine ghesso. Sometimes we will add a simple filler material (cellulose filler) to thicken it.

Palomino finish: Two or more colours or tones, one wiped over the other, to produce a wide variety of finishes.

Wash coat: The thin, semi-transparent light coat applied to wood in order to lighten its natural colour without bleaching and disguise flaws or unmatched wood. A glaze or shader is applied over wash coat.

Scuff sanding: Very light sanding to scuff the surface of wood, sealer or paint and eliminate grit in preparation for a following coating.

Transparency: A transparent, tinted coating of varnish or paint mainly applied over solid colours to build up a shimmering and deep,

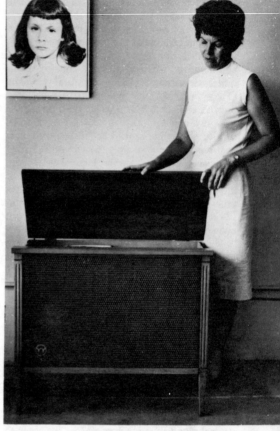

A wash coat and a glaze, rather than bleaching, gave this record player a French walnut finish.

high-gloss finish on oriental-styled pieces. Other transparencies are used to subtly age or alter the tone of painted finishes.

Rubbing compound: An abrasive paste ready-mixed for use and available at paint stores. Used for fine polishing of gloss finishes, especially the oriental styles.

Primer: A coating to prepare the wood or metal for following colour coats.

Sealer: A coating to shut in stains which could bleed from an old finish into a new paint coat.

68

Above left: Are you tired of the dull, dreary appearance of the family's TV set? Consider a conversion job.

Above: Look how an easily-applied antique white finish glamorizes and refreshes the tired old mahogany!

Left: 'Palomino' treatment turned this mahogany plywood door into a spacious, useful coffee table.

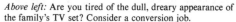

Scotch-Brite pads and steel wool: Steel wool splinters and leaves a greyish dirty look when used on flat paint or any other finish that is not smooth and hard, such as varnish or enamel. But even on light-coloured enamels, steel wool will often as not grey out and ruin the pure colour of the finish. Scotch-Brite pads made of nylon and abrasive are available both in the moderately coarse 'general purpose' type (which is similar to No. 000 steel wool) and the 'ultra-fine' type (which is as fine as No. 0000 steel wool). These work faster and more smoothly, leaving no residue or splinters. Use Scotch-Brite pads for every operation where you would have used steel wool formerly.

Brushing lacquer: Lacquer both clear and in colours that is slower drying than the type made for spraying. Can be brushed on as a finish.

Crackle: We mean only the type of pattern produced on purpose when we make the paint separate, leaving fine openings in a way that simulates old, crackled paint.

Wrinkle: The effect seen when lacquer is sprayed over paint or enamel or varnish. The lacquer thinner mixed with the lacquer eats into the other finish and lifts it, producing wrinkles.

Experiment! With scrap lumber, test and explore paints, enamels, metallics, colours of all kinds.

To save time and avoid sloppiness, organize all finishing materials before starting a new job.

Characteristics of Standard Paints

Interior oil-base paints and enamels are thoroughly compatible with all the oil system materials discussed in the previous sections. Oil colours, tinting colours and oil-soluble dry powder colours can be mixed with them.

They are reduced with paint thinner and varnish may be combined with them to give them a hard surface, alter the degree of gloss or make transparencies.

They may be applied in any sequence over each other when the under finish is properly prepared.

For outdoor furniture, the oil-base paints and enamels can be used and coated with a transparency or clear application of a weather-proof oil-base finish such as spar varnish or polyurethane varnish. Or enamels made to withstand weathering, such as marine enamels, can be used.

The marine enamels of the oil-base type can be used anywhere you want an extraordinarily tough finish.

Do not work from large containers of finishes. Pour what you need into paper cups or tin cans.

70

For patching of nail holes and small flaws, use a cellulose filler, grain filler or stopping.

Use plastic wood to fill large open joints, as often found on inexpensive, unfinished frames.

Preparation is half the battle. To ready the TV set, remove the doors, all screw-held hardware.

After proper preparation of the surface, the oil-base paints and enamels can be applied successfully over any other kind of old finish, usually without removing that old finish first. Just be sure it is intact.

Interior water-soluble paints vary considerably in type and quality and in the use we can get from them. It is not necessary to buy expensive paints of this type for many applications, particularly when ghesso or clear coatings or transparencies will be laid over them. They do not intermix with the oil system materials. Tinting colours of most makes will tone them adequately. Water-soluble dry powder pigments or other water colouring agents can be used also. Experimentation is the only key to what can and cannot be mixed with these paints, since the manufacturers produce many and varied types.

In general, they can be combined (as we shall do for certain purposes) with glue, plaster of Paris, fillers like Alabastine, chalk, cake and vegetable food colourings. For special pur-

Working with the grain, carefully sand all raw wood surfaces, using progressively finer paper.

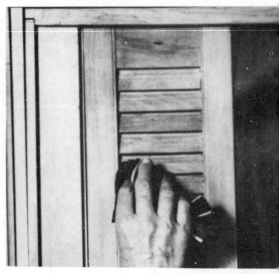

After sanding, wipe off dust with rag moistened with paint thinner. Be sure to get into cracks.

poses, where we will utilize their inability to properly combine with oil system materials, we will make them combine in a somewhat improper but handsome manner with almost anything, including shellac, varnish and other improbable materials. Heavy-bodied, they can be textured for arty effects. Quick-drying, easy to apply with brush, roller, spray gun, spatula or whatever, they are ideal for much of our work with painted finishes.

Application over old finishes varies. Some types can be applied and some cannot. Good quality brands of the latex, vinyl and lucite types will adhere to most old finishes after the finish is properly prepared. They can be applied directly to raw wood also. Usually, they can be applied in much heavier coats than oil-base finishes. While some are not formulated to withstand wear, stains or hardly any liquids at all, coatings of clear varnish or transparencies will make them tough and durable.

Enamels are so much like varnish that they should be thought of as coloured varnish. Thus

For raw wood, apply clear shellac sealer coat. Use clean brush not previously used for paint.

After scraping, use lacquer or paint thinner to clean oil, dirt, wax, etc., from the old finish.

Cover depressions in finish with a paste filler made from cellulose filler and sealed with knotting or sealer, or varnish.

Old finish may not require removal. However, do scrape off any loose paint, lacquer, varnish, etc.

all the characteristics of varnish can be applied to them. Cheap enamel is notoriously miserable to use. Thin, slow-drying, drippy, poorly pigmented cheap enamel should be avoided at all times for all purposes. Quality enamel is heavy-bodied and thoroughly opaque with good and true colouring. It is available in fast-drying types and handles very well.

Lacquer enamels and regular enamels available in aerosol pressure cans for spray-type application vary greatly depending upon the manufacturer.

In most cases, if not all, the amount of coverage stated on the label is somewhat exaggerated. One type tested was labelled with a claimed coverage of 80 square feet under normal circumstances and actually covered 20 square feet to the last drop. The surface was ideal for coverage and the colour a grey-green which ordinarily covers very well. Unfortunately, this peculiar measuring system is applied by many manufacturers of aerosol lacquers and enamels. The paint people also apply it in the case of water-soluble interior wall paints which always seem to require at least twice as much as the label indicates. However, let's get what use we can from these little spray cans. Use them on small areas such as legs, outdoor furniture and other intricate metal or wire assemblies.

There are on the market many kinds of one-coaters, synthetic fast finishes and other varieties to be used in place of standard paints and enamels. Some of these work very well. Some should be used to lather their manufacturers. Experiment at will with these. They will not be discussed here, however, in order to keep our work simple and basic. Remember again, this is a system that is actually basic to all finishing. Learn the system first, get the fundamentals mastered and then explore and explore.

In general, the painted finishes are much easier to work with than the clear finishes. This is particularly true of the solid colour coats which conceal all flaws and repair work. As often as not, you will not have to strip off the old finish. You can do your repair work with a carefree disregard for craftsmanship with full confidence that all hammer tracks, open joints, bent finishing nails and the like can be camouflaged easily. Just be sure the framework is made solid, that gouges and cracks are filled and all are sanded down smoothly. After that, it is a simple enough matter to apply some kind of painted finish. If the colour does not turn out quite right, or if spots show through, just work over it until you are satisfied.

The basic steps in producing a good painted finish are:

1. Careful preparation of the piece so that the paint will adhere and lay on smoothly, requiring only a few coats.

2. Use of clear and pure colour that you do not muddy up with a dirty brush or allow to be disfigured with dust and lint.

3. Proper mixing of materials, neither too thin nor too thick, so that the paint goes on without overlaps, streaks, thin spots, drips

With fine sandpaper, level off repaired finish to provide smooth, even surface for new coating.

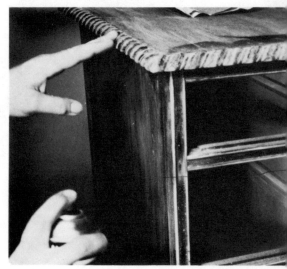

After sanding, spray or brush on a sealing coat to prevent bleeding, especially near end grain.

or runs and is still thick enough to permit fine sanding or rubbing when required.

4. Producing a smooth, flawless surface, either through finish brushing or rubbing and polishing with abrasives.

Several moderately thin coats are much better than one heavy one. Drying is more thorough and the several coats build up a tougher finish less subject to cracking and peeling and altogether more durable than a single, heavy coating.

The thin coat dries faster and thus reduces the chances of dust and lint settling on the wet surface.

Take good care of your brushes and materials. Do not work directly from large cans of paint, but pour into other containers what you need and keep the lip of the can clean so it can be properly closed. Do not muddy up your coloured paints and enamels by dipping from one to the other when mixing.

Clean your brushes after work is done and keep them clean and soft. Store them wet in the correct thinner during intermittent use, but store them clean and dry between projects.

Preparation for Painting

Pieces to be coated with opaque finishes require repair and patching that is strictly functional and that is all. Do not concern yourself with matching woods or making airtight joints when you patch up holes. Do dig out charred wood from burns and spots softened by acids or stains, etc. Be sure the wood is solid all over and smoothly sanded with No. 1½ and 1 finishing paper. Fill up all depressions and cracks with stopping, cellulose filler or plastic wood. While sanding across the grain will not disfigure a piece to be painted, do not get any bad habits started. Sand with the grain. Make this a reflex and you will be a happier finisher.

The manners in which we prepare raw, unfinished or stripped wood and wood with an old finish on it differ in several ways. Let us look at the method of preparing raw wood first.

When sealer is dry, scuff sand lightly. On unfinished wood like this, good seal is important.

Many unfinished hardwoods can be primed directly like this, without requiring a sealing coat.

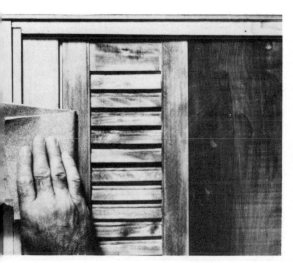

Preparation of unfinished wood

To simplify, let us now refer to oil paint and enamel just as paint. When we mean water-soluble interior paints, we will call them water paints.

Both paint and water paint can be applied directly to raw wood without first priming or sealing. It is not always best, but it can be done. In effect, any coat you put on raw wood first becomes the primer coat and can be considered a sealer, too, unless the character of the wood requires special sealing material. But such cases only complicate an otherwise pleasant and simple job.

Now the primer, or first coat, has a job to do and that is to soak into the wood and dry there so that saturation will be even when you apply a subsequent coating. Saturation usually is not even with the first coat.

A sealer accomplishes much the same purpose. Despite all you will hear about priming and sealing, you may go on for years just daubing paint on wood and never have a bit of trouble. However, it is practical and economical to treat the first coat of paint or water paint as a primer-sealer. And sometimes it pays dividends to actually seal the wood before painting.

Priming the wood: If you are using an enamel for the finish, then use an enamel undercoater first. Work it well into the wood and, when it is dry, scuff sand it before applying the first coat of enamel. The undercoat will help fill small grain pits but should not be used thickly in any effort to replace filler.

If you are using a paint other than enamel, the enamel undercoater still may be used as a primer—or thin out a flat paint and brush it well into the wood. Gloss and semi-gloss paints do not work as well for priming, for they require more sanding to get a surface that the next coat will stick to without slipping.

If, after the primer coat is dry, you see that in some areas the wood has drunk up the primer excessively, it is best to recoat those areas and let them dry out before going on. A surface that will take the finish coats of paint

If primer soaks in too much in spots, apply a second coat before putting on first colour coat.

Sand the primer coat only as much as necessary to remove lumps and other spots. Use fine paper.

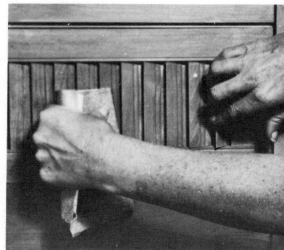

evenly without sucking it down in spots will surely be easier to work with and may require only one or two coats in place of three.

If you are working with water paint (and recall now that we mean water-soluble paints such as latex), prime the surface with a moderately thinned-out coating. Adding too much water will cut down the sticking ability of the paint and you accomplish nothing. As a matter of fact, with most of these water paints you shouldn't bother with priming. Just paint the piece and be done with it.

Sealing the wood: Sappy wood, knotty wood and woods with natural staining colours in them (like some pieces of mahogany, for example) must be sealed to avoid considerable trouble.

A coat of thinned-down shellac, mixed one part shellac to five parts denatured alcohol or shellac thinner, should be brushed or sprayed on the wood. Extra coats applied to knots and sappy streaks help considerably. The shellac will seal down the juices and prevent them from

working up into the wet paint where they can discolour it. Knotting is also available.

When the shellac coat has dried well (anywhere up to two hours and more, depending on how thick you actually mix it when you get down to it and how many coats you apply), then scuff sand it with $1\frac{1}{2}$ paper. You can tell when the shellac is dry enough by touch. If it gums or seems anything but willing to powder when you sand it, it is not dry.

After sealing, there is no good reason to apply a primer coat, since the shellac will harden the wood fibres and permit an even saturation by the paint. However, it does no harm to give it a primer coat on general principles.

A shellac coating also makes for much smoother painting, since it provides a fairly hard surface. It is good practice to seal woods with shellac before working with any kind of paint. Water paints? Well, here you must try it out. Some of them are of too watery a consistency, so that they do not stick well to shellac or any other finish. The better grades will stick very well indeed. Since the shellac is inexpen-

Paint is of right consistency if it does not run when it is brushed on a clean vertical surface.

Don't overload brush so that paint runs off. Start at the side, not the middle of a panel.

sive, eliminates any need for a primer coat (almost always) and makes for easier, smoother painting, it is ideal to use. It can mean that often one coat of paint will serve where otherwise two or more would be required.

Keep in mind as you make primers that thinners cut down the sticking quality of paints. Oils will slow down the drying time, but help make them stick.

Also keep in mind that woods vary greatly in the amount of liquid they will soak up; thus you accomplish more sealing soft woods like pine than you do sealing woods like oak.

Filling open-grain wood: It is much easier, far less expensive and gives a much more durable finish if you fill open-grain woods with paste filler rather than with paint (with the exception of ghesso, which we will discuss farther on). Apply the filler in the usual way, and, when it is dry, sand the surface well. Then seal it with shellac before painting.

If the piece is to receive a semi-transparent wash coat and glaze, then you must be a little more careful in preparing the wood. There will be no heavy-bodied opaque finish to conceal major flaws or extremely wild combinations of wood.

The wash coat will even out the average variations in colour and grain of similar woods. Be more particular in patching and patch with putty coloured to match the wood as it is raw. Remember that the wash coat is much like a shading or colour toning coat and conceals only as tinted plastic or glass might.

Sealing is far more important when the wood requires it, as we explained. As for priming, suit yourself. Experiment with various kinds of wood and decide which is easiest for you. Much will depend upon the way you apply finish coats. After all, there are two kinds of painters. Some prime and some do not prime raw wood. Are you going to be a primer or an anti-primer? Experiment and do what comes naturally.

In those rare and unhappy cases where colours bleed through even a coat of shellac and into a first coat of paint, you must stop the

Work paint into the hard spots first, using a small brush. Fill in the large, flat areas later.

An egg or fruit crate makes a good support for painted work. Protect the floor with newspapers.

bleeding with more than shellac. Alcohol-proof bartop varnish will usually do. Apply a coat, sand it and carry on.

Preparation of old finishes

Old finishes must be cleaned to remove wax, grease, oil (such as furniture polish) and dirt. They must be sanded to cut off the oxidation and loose material to provide a solid base for the new finish.

The old surfaces must be restored to a smooth enough character to permit use of only one or two coats of finish. Leaving chipped out depressions and the like will make it necessary to either pile extra coats of paint on the piece or patch the depressions before applying the final top coat of finish.

Cleaning the old finish: Commercial cleaners are available and work well enough. However, the materials on hand for finishing will do. Test the finish first to determine what has to be done. Try some No. 1 finishing paper on it. Wax will load up the paper fast with a

dirty yellowish paste. Old varnish will powder quickly if it has no wax on it. It will not load up the paper. Old lacquer will also powder, but produces a finer dust. Old varnish and old lacquer have their individual characteristic odours. Learn them.

To remove wax, oil and grease, scrub the piece well, using a Scotch-Brite pad (or steel wool) soaked moderately with lacquer thinner. Lacquer thinner will not soften old varnish or lacquer. It will tend to soften relatively new lacquer and, to a lesser extent, newer varnishes of most kinds. It will not soften old paint or enamel. Yes, lacquer thinner, if soaked long enough on an old finish, will begin to eat into it. But the time spent in scrubbing is not nearly long enough.

If, after trying a little thinner, you find it is raising the Old Harry with the finish, stop using it. Change over to paint thinner and continue cleaning. In either case, you will find that a little wax residue still packs into the finishing paper. But continue sanding until the surface powders.

Pay particular attention to the corners, as paint has a tendency to soak into open end grain here.

Start a cabinet top by painting the trim first. Work rapidly so that paint sets evenly all over.

Beads invariably form on undersides of painted surfaces. Wipe them off with moistened brush.

Don't forget to paint the inside posts of drawers. They will show when the latter are opened.

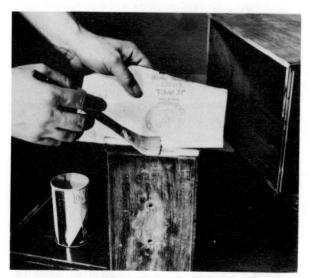

Since drawers are kept closed most of the time. their sides need only be painted an inch or two.

Heavy coat of paint on edges of drawer is often cause of binding. Plane or sand for proper fit.

Get even better acquainted with the cleaning solvents. You will find that you can prepare a mixture of liquid paint remover and lacquer thinner and use it on very old, hard finishes without lifting or wrinkling. Judicious use of variations of this mixture (strong or weak) will

First paint a border around a surface. Then fill in, feathering to border but not over the edges.

Start finishing strokes well within the outer edges, and lift brush smoothly at end of run.

speed up cleaning of old work. It also will help remove surface oxidation and slightly soften the top of an old finish (when mixed just strong enough to do so) so that you then can brush the very little bit of paste produced over the surface, filling hairline cracks, bare spots and the like. When this softened finish has dried out well, you can sand it and proceed.

Alcohol, naphtha and other solvents also will clean furniture. So will carbon tetrachloride, but do not use it. Carbon tet, while noninflammable, is lethal. Do not ever use carbon tet. It gets into the body, stays there (in the liver), accumulates and kills—or so it has been reported.

Preparing chipped and worn surfaces: If old paint, varnish or lacquer is flaking off, chipping and the like, and the surface is filled with potholes, craters and valleys, you must level it off before proceeding. Sanding is required for the worst cases. Sand and fill with cellulose filler.

The questionable cases—those that look bad but seem within hope—can be patched up without sanding down the whole surface.

Use wood surfacing filler and/or wood stopping to fill holes, cracks and gouges where raw wood is exposed. To fill up the chipped out areas, first go over the area with a putty knife and a steel wire brush to remove any flakes of paint that are loose. Then prepare a filling compound and spread it over the surface with a putty knife.

One adequate filler is made by blending a cellulose filler or a grain filler with lacquer sanding sealer to form a heavy, creamy, paint-like paste. This dries rapidly and must be used quickly. Keep it soft by adding more lacquer sealer or thinner if necessary.

Another filler to be used, especially under water paint, is made by combining heavy, thick water paint with cellulose filler or Alabastine. Do not mix the paint paste with the liquid. Pour off the liquid and use the paste thick. Leftover paint that has had time to thicken works well. Mix up some filler and water thicker than is called for normally. After it has become creamy smooth, combine it with water paint. Use more paint than filler. Spread this

Paints can be blended directly without preliminary mixing in a can. Apply lighter colours first.

Tinting colours come in squeeze bottle, can and tube. Stipple while first colour is wet.

Gradations of colours from an intense shade to a subtle hue are obtainable with surface blending.

Surface blending of wet paint requires thorough brushing. Cross brushing is frequently helpful.

over the surface to fill. Do not use based filler only for this purpose. It will not work.

In all cases, there are exceptions. Experi-ment and discover what you can and cannot do to different types of old finishes. (When in doubt, sand the old finish off or strip it off.)

82

After being primed, hardwood frame may need only single finish coat. Sand lightly to remove dust.

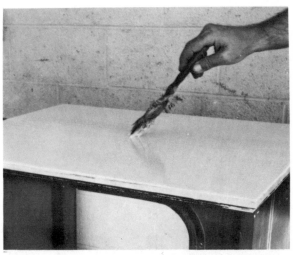

For smooth paint or enamel finish, stroke delicately with brush moistened with proper thinner.

If needed for protection, thin coating of varnish can be applied over oil or water-base paint.

Sealing the old finish: After cleaning, and where necessary after filling an old surface, sand it with coarse and fine paper. Wipe the dust off with paint thinner on a tack rag. This will dry out in minutes, and you are ready to proceed with sealing.

Shellac in the standard four-pound cut is the traditional and common sealer for this purpose. (Four-pound cut is a technical phrase that indicates the standard proportion of solid shellac to solvent as prepared by the manufacturer. Other cuts can be used.)

Reduce four-pound cut shellac with alcohol or shellac thinner or methylated spirit in a proportion of about five to one (again a standard practice). Brush the prepared shellac over the old finish thoroughly. It will dry out rather quickly (about half an hour). Then give it a second coat. Let this dry for an hour or two until it feels dry to the touch and does not drag when you sand—as you will—with fine paper.

The shellac hardens the old surface, binds it up and prevents the colour in it from soaking into the new finish. It also makes a smooth surface which permits easier coverage and the use of smaller amounts in painting.

Varnish may also be used to seal old finishes. Use a thin mix and be sure it is thoroughly dry before proceeding.

Spray cans are ideal for scroll work, grilles, wicker and wire chairs. Paint goes on evenly.

Deep, narrow areas, hard to reach with brushes, are finished in short order with aerosol sprays.

Wood shutters are difficult to paint with conventional brushes, but are easy with spray can.

A common flush door is converted quickly into a coffee table by addition of four screw-on legs.

Commercial sealers are on the market and can be used. Just be sure you try them first and find out what they will and will not do.

Application of Painted Finishes

Paints and enamels, ghessos, water paints, palominos and wash coats can be applied with

Coated with clear varnish, the grain character of the door's light mahogany finish is retained.

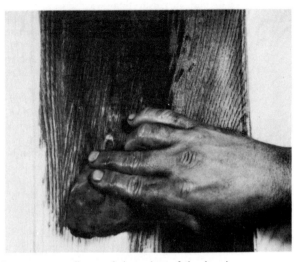

In some surroundings, a darker colour of the door is desirable. It can be wiped on readily by hand.

The filler colour has been laid on a little too heavily here. It obscures the grain of the wood.

brush, roller, spray gun, spray can and, in the case of ghesso, with a spatula or putty knife.

Two objectives should be kept clearly in mind: (1) the appearance of the finished product and (2) the functional use required of the finished product. To insure a finish that will serve you adequately in both requirements, keep work samples in process ahead of the actual processing of your furniture.

Trying out colour mixtures, textures, coatings, sanding, etc., before you work your project will pay handsome dividends. Will a coat of paint on the piece of furniture absorb an oil glaze? Will it permit smooth, even distribution of the glaze when you brush it or wipe it down, as when doing an antique white piece? There is only one way to be sure, because of the many varied qualities of paint: Test it on a work sample. And this rule applies to all other matters as well. Where with quality varnish certain generally true statements can be made and routine practices indicated, with paints this is not the case. You must find paints that will do what you want them to do and stick with them.

Oil-base paints and enamels: Unless otherwise indicated, everything we discuss about oil-base paints will be applicable to enamels, pigmented (coloured) varnish that you prepare yourself for transparencies or opaque finishes and any other combinations of oil-base paints, enamels or varnishes designed to make opaque, semi-opaque or transparent 'paint' coats. We will concern ourselves only with the faster-drying types. This means paints that set dust-free under normal warm and dry conditions in 15 minutes to half an hour. They are dry to the light touch in one hour or less and can be used in four to eight hours. Drying speed is essential in furniture finishing only in terms of the initial dust-free setup so that the surface does not require endless sanding to get the dust particles out of it.

Three moderate coatings of paint should be your standard of quality. While the entire coating will be no thicker than you might apply in two passes, the durability and workability and the final appearance are superior when thinner coats are applied one at a time and processed separately than if you try to do the job in one quick thick coating. Just as we learned with varnish, the thinner coats produce quality work. The heavy coats produce headaches and inferior end products.

Some paints come thin enough in the can. Others must be reduced with paint thinner. The exact proportion varies from paint to paint. What you want is a creamy, opaque liquid that brushes easily, covers well, does not run off like water and will not pile up, lap or drag. When you can brush a creamy paint on the shellacked surface of a board that stands upright and the paint sticks, covers and does not run, then you have it about right.

Do not overload your brush or roller. Take enough paint so that it flows out of the brush because of the slight pressure you apply, not because it wants to.

Following the same good practice you learned with clear finishing, brush in the difficult spots first. Get your edges and inset panel margins. Get into carvings and turnings. Do the inside edges of scroll work first.

For an open-grain finish, brush a glaze over the base coat. Let it set; then wipe off carefully.

Lay the brush strokes on in long straight sweeps when you do the flat surface. Work the end of a table top, for example, by doing only that area a few inches from the edge and get the edge done well. Then do the other end. Before the paint sets up, complete the swath by painting the full length, but without slapping the brush over the ends. Look under the trim and top for drips and wipe them off while still wet. If you find drips after the paint has begun to set up or is dry, cut them off.

Overlaps, runs and other irregularities or flaws should be corrected after the paint is dry. Lightly sand down any raised spots, using fine-grade paper dry or wet. Touch up missed spots or thin spots with a little paint and let them dry; then sand the spots before proceeding.

When the first coat of paint is dry, scuff-sand it with fine paper such as a 220 Wet-or-Dry type, using a little water for lubricant. (Do not use soapy water!)

Following coats are applied in the same

What finishing can do! Left side of oak piece is glazed with burnt umber under base coat of ivory.

To remove excess filler, first wipe across the grain, then with it to pick up loose droplets.

manner. However, as you now try to produce smoother and smoother surfaces, you may find that the paint is setting up before you can brush it out as much as you wish. Wet your brush slightly with paint thinner and work over the paint. But be careful! Do not brush the paint off or work it over too much. Enamel is particularly troublesome in this respect. Do not try to cover more than one surface at a time with enamel. Brush each surface completely and finish it off before going on.

After the first coat, each single coat of paint can be wiped off while still wet—or before complete drying—by using paint thinner and a rag. This may be necessary at times when you just cannot get it smooth, or where the colour is not right. Rather than fret and frantically try to wet and re-wet the paint to make it behave, wipe it off and then check your paint. Is it too thick? Too thin? Has the weather suddenly changed since yesterday when the same paint worked perfectly? Or should you be out fishing

and relaxing instead of getting yourself, your workroom and half the house splattered with paint?

Mood is important. Do not push yourself and do not take it out on the furniture when you would rather be pounding someone's skull into concrete. Furniture is designed to serve mankind. It is without malice. Treat it at least as well as you do your prize beagle hound.

If you smoke while painting, do not blame the furniture for the ashes that fall on to that perfectly smooth enamel coating at the last critical second.

The finish coats: The final coat or coats must give the protection needed for the piece and permit a finish lustre that is right. We have several processes that we can use to achieve the finish results desired:

1. Polishing and rubbing.
2. Selection of a final coat that is flat or glossy.

Although made of high-grade plywood, this cabinet did not look bold enough. Treatment follows.

To open the grain of the wood, it was scrubbed with a clean steel brush having sharp bristles.

3. Application of a clear finish over the paint.

4. Choice of a paint in the beginning that will be right for the final coat.

Enamels are available that are tough and will resist stains, beverages, heat, etc. They are gloss or semi-gloss usually. While enamel applied expertly will have a good-looking sheen and a smooth surface, the best results are obtained by rubbing down the final coat much as we would varnish or lacquer. However, steel wool cannot be used on light-coloured enamel because it dirties it with grey. For a high-gloss finish, work the final coat with wet finishing paper such as Tri-M-Ite, using water to lubricate. The No. 400 grade is normally coarse enough to begin with. If not, use a paper in the 300 or 200 series as required and follow with finer papers to the 400. If you rub properly with 400 paper and water, working in straight lines and not letting your arm swing in arcs, you will produce a moderately lustrous surface without further rubbing. The 600 paper worked the same way after the 400 will produce a fine, lustrous sheen.

Rubbing compounds ready prepared and used to polish the surface will produce an even higher gloss finish. The natural gloss of unrubbed enamels, like unrubbed varnishes and lacquers, is always garish and is not handsome. The polishing process—even when producing a high gloss—achieves good-looking finish results.

A gentle white scouring powder worked in straight lines like compound will produce a lustrous finish especially good for table tops in antique white.

The Scotch-Brite ultrafine pad can be used by itself or with scouring powder or compounds, but this can discolour the lighter finishes a little. It depends on the finish whether or not the colour will come off with cleaning. Test first.

Paints are available in lustres ranging from flat to gloss. Select the one you want. Do not plan on rubbing the final coat of paint. If you want the high-gloss rubbed look, use enamel,

The technique is to brush from the centre out to the edges. This prevents splintering and tearing.

Now comes a base coat, followed by a glaze. This is wiped down; only the grain pits remain dark.

not paint. Enamel can be used as a final coat over most paints, so this offers no problem.

To get a smooth final coat of flat or semi-gloss paint applied properly, work the coating before it down to perfection. Apply as many coats as necessary and sand them with fine paper (such as 400 Tri-M-Ite) until you get a perfectly smooth, even surface. Then, for the finish coating, thin out your paint considerably and brush it on in a dust-free place with utmost care. When dry, it will have the lustre you want and will need no further processing.

To secure a bar-top quality finish which will withstand alcohol and hard usage, apply a coat or two of water-clear bar-top varnish over the paint. Rub it and polish it as we did with clear varnish for natural finishes. The varnish can be tinted with the same oil-base paint used on the piece to produce a transparency that will cut any reflection in the finish, help to cover and, in the case of flat varnish, will look just like the flat paint. Transparencies made with gloss varnish will produce a shimmering appearance like deep water. The slight colour tinting of the

varnish will also prevent discolouration from the natural yellowing of the varnish.

Remember that enamel is varnish with colour pigment in it. Therefore, if you mix colour or oil-base paint with varnish, you get an effect like enamel, but by making it yourself, you can control the lustre to produce flat finishes. Experiment! Always experiment first.

Do not apply lacquers or other sealer-finishes and the like now found on the market over paint or enamel unless you make a thorough test first. Otherwise you may wind up with a wrinkled and discoloured mess.

Transparencies made by tinting varnish with oil colours or paint can be used to achieve extraordinarily beautiful painted finishes. By building coat upon coat of these transparencies and sanding and rubbing properly in between to get rid of dust and level out the surface of the finish itself, you can produce deep, lustrous colours that are like the finest oriental lacquers. The transparencies can be made of the same colour or each one can be varied in order to achieve many different effects.

The contrast between light and dark can be further accentuated by sanding the surface lightly.

Light colours can be wiped over dark base coats for interesting effects. Here, white over black.

Heavy-bodied ghesso is brushed on in straight lines to produce unusual straight-grain effect.

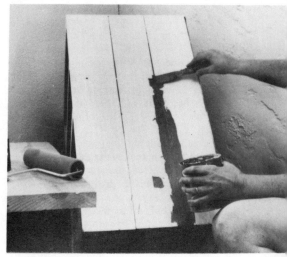

Open joints between boards can be filled easily with ghesso and water-filler paste. Push in well.

In place of coating with a green, for example, building a finish of transparencies made of alternating coats of blue and yellow will result in a green that is almost gem-like in quality.

Endless variations and subtle tonings and shadings can be made with these transparencies—and they can be applied over natural wood or a painted surface.

Ghesso can be applied with a brush or roller, or a combination of the two. Putty knife is all right, too.

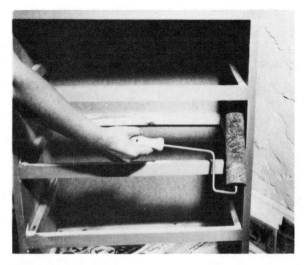

If manipulated with imagination, a paint roller can be got into the most improbable places.

Allow the first ghesso coat to dry for several hours; then sand it to a smooth, even finish.

Transparencies also are most practical when used to age out a finish or soften the colour. Small amounts of metallic powders like gold and silver, when used skilfully, either in the final transparency or under other tinted transparencies, add an unusual character to the finish.

Water paints: The water-soluble paints are applied much as the oil-base paints. Prepare a mixture that brushes or rolls on smoothly. Use a little water on a brush or roller to get a perfectly smooth final coating or to make the paint workable if it sets up too fast.

Sand between coats with paper. Because these paints set up so rapidly, there is seldom any problem with dust settling on them. Therefore sanding is held to a minimum between coats and scuff-sanding is almost always enough. Just be sure if you have a rough coat that you sand it smooth before applying the second coat.

Many of these paints can be applied much more thickly than oil-base paints but, even so, two coats (with the second coat thinned down to be creamy) work better than one.

Transparencies made with varnish and colour (or with paint as we just discussed) can be applied over water paints. Varnishes, paints

91

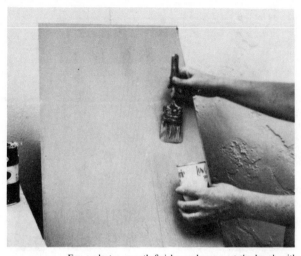

For a plaster smooth finish on ghesso, wet the brush with water and go over it before it sets.

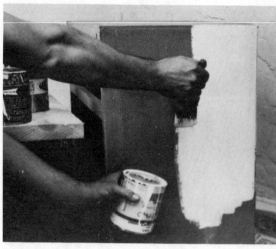

Brush on the final coat of ghesso evenly with a medium-size brush. Avoid thick and thin spots.

For a textured ghesso, add the dry powder directly to vinyl or latex paint; mix well.

Seal off on old finish with shellac, and sand it well. Use ghesso freely and get it into carvings.

and enamels also can be laid over them where needed for a finish coat. Since many of these water paints will not stand up under the kind of abuse given to coffee and dining tables, it is best not to use them for such applications—but if you do for one reason or another, and want

Dry, the ghesso has a somewhat coarse surface. Sand this lightly for an interesting texture.

After gilding the inner border of frame, paint and tone the rest of the surface with oil colours.

to make them conform to rigid specifications, then top them off with varnish or a varnish transparency.

These water-soluble paints can be fine-sanded to produce good finish results, but do not try to rub them with steel wool or compounds. If they are waterproof, you can rub them down with scouring powder.

For most painted finishes, the oil-base interior fast-dry paints are best. The water paints work well for special applications, as we shall see, but for standard work, it is best to stick with the oil-base paints.

The palomino finishes: If you sealed a sheet of bleached mahogany veneer, then wiped a burnt umber coloured filler over it, both filling the open grain and glazing the entire surface to produce a light brown wood, you would have a result that has the characteristics of a palomino finish; that is, two-tone with the darker colour wiped into the grain or into the depressions made when you texture wood one way or another. It makes a very attractive finish.

The basic palomino (from which the name was adapted to mean all kinds of two-tone finishes involving a glazing operation) is mahogany painted and glazed to look lighter than the natural wood and resemble fruitwood in a general way.

The process is simple enough. After preparing an unfinished surface and brushing out the grain with a wire brush to open it up, apply a coat of paint (mixed to a neutral wood shade) and be careful not to fill up the grain of the wood. When this is dry and scuff-sanded, apply a darker glaze (usually a burnt umber) and wipe it down evenly so that the resulting colour resembles light walnut or light brown mahogany. Over this a coat of clear finish is applied. All the natural grain patterns are concealed except the pit pattern itself, which takes the darker glaze (or filler). Yet the over-all appearance is so realistic that when you see these pieces in stores you are probably not aware that they are painted finishes at all. They appear to be natural wood.

Driftwood is processed in the same way. Walnut is painted a grey or soft bluish colour and then a compatible shade is glazed over it.

93

The unusual ghesso finish of this handsome frame excites comment from all who see it for the first time.

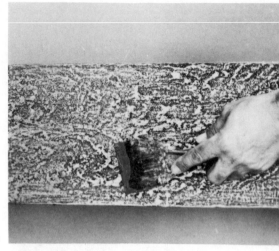

When partially set, heavy ghesso can be textured with a putty knife to form intricate patterns.

Smoky colours, pickled effects, waterlogged tones and the like all are made this way.

Any open grain wood can be given a palomino finish. Experiment first with the combination of colours to see what the result will be. When you have your colours right, then just go ahead and apply the paint coat first. When it is dry, apply the glaze. Then top the glaze off, after drying, with a clear finish. If you use oil-base paint for a glaze, it will dry hard and you will not even need the clear top coat.

Another type of palomino is much used in the decorator trade. Rather than wiping colour into the open grain, woods like ash, fir, redwood and oak are sandblasted to cut away the softer porous material, leaving the entire grain pattern. A coat of paint is applied over all. When dry, a second colour or darker shade of the first is then wiped on to achieve interesting effects. The second coat may be wiped down well, leaving only a little colour against the grain ridges, or it may be worked out like a glaze, leaving some colour over all.

A wire brush can be used to texture wood. Scrub across the grain of softwood and with the grain of hardwood until the softer material is cut away. Seal the wood with shellac and then apply a coat of paint. Follow the paint with a wiped-on colour.

If you use a roller to apply the second colour to wood that has been textured it will coat mostly just the higher, raised grain surfaces for a bold effect. The roller also can be used to good purpose when coating a flat area that is to get just a glaze to colour the open grain afterwards. (We will discuss the texturing of wood in more detail later under Specialty Finishes.)

The base coat of a palomino can be applied easily with spray equipment. In fact, this is the simplest way to do it if you have such equipment.

Wash coat and glaze: This finish is the first cousin of the palomino. The wash coat, however, is never opaque, but rather a more or less transparent light toner that conceals flaws and unmatched wood or simply provides an even colouring. Over this, a darker tone is glazed or shaded to produce the light wood colour desired. The wash coat and glaze are often

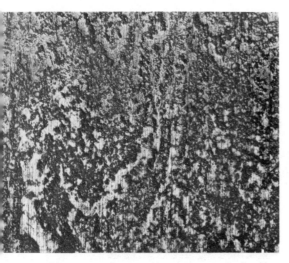

Other means of wet-texturing gesso are wire brushing, sanding with coarse paper and combing.

Cross-hatch and plaid effects in gesso are obtained by brushing them directly on to the work.

applied to close-grained woods and to soft-woods like pine and poor-quality cabinet woods like gum, fir and so on.

Mahogany is 'bleached' easily by applying a light-toned wash coat made of yellow ochre, burnt sienna and a touch of burnt umber which are milked down with white—but not too much white, for we must retain colour tone. When this is dry a light tone of burnt umber with a little yellow ochre added is glazed over carefully. Presto! Light mahogany. The popular light 'tan', fruitwoods, French walnuts, provincials, etc., are made with this process a good bit of the time.

It is wise to seal the wood before giving it a wash coat of paint. This will provide an even surface and make for equal saturation. Commercially, wash coats are sprayed on wood.

You may think of a wash coat as a transparency, colour toning, shading, glazing, or even wipe-on staining. Any of these approaches will get results. At times, your purpose is to conceal flaws; at others it is to get a light neutral wood tone over dark wood so that you have, in effect, a light piece of wood. Then you wipe colour over it rather than staining as you do with the raw wood.

The base coat for both palomino and wash coat-glaze finishes should be one that the second coat will not soak into. The second coat must wipe on the first and wipe off if you wish to remove it. Therefore, it's best to use a coloured varnish or a thin enamel for the base coat. The wiping coat of colour can be paint, oil pigment, coloured varnish or water paint—whatever will produce the results you want. Experiment to find the result that satisfies you.

It is very important to keep the colour of the base coat for the palomino finish or the wash coat for the wash coat-glaze process as pure as possible. By this we mean that if you milk it down too much with white to make that neutral, light wood shade, then the second colour glazed over it will produce nothing more than something like burnt umber over white which, for example, is terrible. Keep the neutral base colour to the yellow side and you will be safe.

The proportions given for neutral toners in the sections on staining and colour toning apply to the wash coat colours as well.

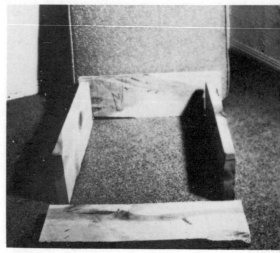

Dragging a dry brush over partially set ghesso piles it into unusual contours and grain shapes.

Good use for ghesso: To make rough lumber suitable as base for a large cushion. It's a trick!

Now a wash coat may be other than a neutral tone. A wash coat of yellow ochre or light maple colour, for example, is often used to improve the appearance of pines or maples, much as a shader would. You may want to wash coat oak with a thin burnt umber before glazing with white or you may want to wash coat with grey before glazing with a much lighter blue-grey or hazy purplish grey. Experiment with many colours that please you. Combine strong rich colours as well as the more common 'natural' wood tones.

Use the wash coat and glaze especially to improve inferior mahogany pieces or to change many kinds of wood into the provincial fruit-wood finish. The palomino is the fundamental technique for reproducing the popular 'old world' finishes.

Adding distress marks to palomino or wash coats done in the light 'tan' or fruitwood shades gives a fine antique effect.

The ghesso finish: The ghesso finish is strictly fun. No finishing process offers a wider range of creative pleasure or easy-to-do decorating than this ancient technique. Like so many of our contemporary delights, the ghesso process was invented centuries ago by desperate, harried artisans who had to make something from nothing. Lost in the dust of ancient China is the record of that remarkable craftsman who (probably faced with a choice of producing ornate, superbly-finished furniture out of wood that wouldn't make good orange crates or being boiled in pork fat) came up with ghesso.

Ghesso, once strictly a necessity, no longer serves its original purpose. Now we use the ghesso technique to produce pieces of exceptional beauty and interest or to literally transform cabinetry from humdrum to handsome.

Ghesso is to furniture what fine plaster is to lathing. It is a heavy-bodied paste that dried hard and can be 'plastered' over almost any surface to conceal all flaws and inferior work. With ghesso, an apple crate can be transformed into a finely-finished cabinet as beautiful as any oriental chest.

If you have worked with the water-soluble interior flat wall paints, you will recall that this paint thickens when left exposed in a gallon

96

The magic will be done with paper towels, water-soluble paint and other common materials shown.

Frame is assembled with simple end nailing. No sanding or patching needed, but fill large holes.

container. Some types thicken down without skinning over on top and can be re-used if water is mixed in. This thick paint makes a fine ghesso to be applied with brush, roller or putty knife. We can build a fine, smooth surface or produce a textured surface, as we wish.

We can wipe colours into the still wet ghesso, glaze it after it is dry and coat it with clear finishes or transparencies; we can texture it to imitate sandblasted woods; we can build little decorative 'carvings' with it; we can apply it to raw wood, old finishes or Masonite and other hardboard and we can apply it over paper or cloth. There is just one basic rule to follow to ensure satisfactory results: firm up the cabinetry. Be positive that all joints are solid and that the piece cannot shimmy or shake. Ghesso will not repair furniture and it will not hold loose pieces together. It will crack open anywhere a wobbly joint exists.

Real ghesso, like that used commonly over the years on picture frames, is of no interest to us. Our ghesso will be any of the following:

1. Thick water-soluble paint.

2. Water-soluble paint with Alabastine or cellulose filler or plaster of Paris added.

3. Oil-base (thick) interior flat paint.

When you buy the paint, be sure the dealer does not mix it for you! Pour off the thin liquid on top and let the paint sit open until you have a good thick paste.

Water based filler can be added to water paint to give it more body. Mix the dry powder with water to make a thick paste, heavier than normal. Blend it until it is smooth and free from lumps. Then mix this water paste with water paint. Do not add more than one part water paste to two parts paint. If you try to mix the dry powder directly into the water paint, it will be lumpy and gritty. (We'll do this very thing, however, to produce a special effect discussed under Specialty Finishes.)

Brush the ghesso on raw or sealed wood (or another surface) in a coat about as thick as two pennies. Because of the nature of the thick, fast-setting paint used, brush strokes will remain on the surface. Therefore, brush it out carefully so

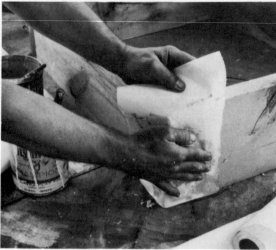

Mix the paint to a slightly thicker than cream consistency and apply initially to the corners.

Press a suitable length of paper towelling into the paint around a corner; paint will hold it.

that fine lines run parallel the long way of the surface.

Coat only one complete surface at a time. Ghesso sets up fast; overworking it will result in stuttering brush marks and the paint will drag. (Any of these irregularities can and will be used to produce textured surfaces, but are not desirable for the smooth, standard ghesso finish.)

Wet your brush with the proper thinner in order to make the final brush passes over a surface and smooth out the paint if necessary.

When this first coat is dry (usually it is best to let it dry overnight at least), sand it carefully with fine paper. Sand in the same direction you brushed to keep the fine lines together. The sanding is done to level off the ghesso and for no other reason. Sand no more than is necessary.

Apply a second coat and let it dry. Sand only as needed with as fine a paper as required to give you the texture you want.

When the second coat is dry and finely sanded, you can apply a top coat, using clear varnish or a transparency. If the paint you used to make the ghesso is a type that will stand up

to the requirement demanded in terms of usage, you need not give it a top coating. Most ghesso finishes are glazed to produce the antique effect so much in vogue.

Glazing ghesso: Glazing with a brush produces fine lines on a surface, as we observed with the clear finishes. The ghesso already has these lines brushed or sanded into it. Thus the glazing job is very simple. Brush the glaze on, brush it down for effect and let it dry.

A glaze can be brushed into the ghesso, mixing with it, or it can be brushed on to the ghesso, not mixing in. Be sure your glaze does what you want it to do, not what happens by accident.

Oil-base ghessos dry out with a surface that will not soften up when you glaze with an oil-type glaze or thinned-down oil paint. But many of the water paint ghessos, even when dry, will soften up when the oil glaze is applied. To prevent this, seal the ghesso first with a very light, dry coating of lacquer sanding sealer, sprayed on from a gun or an aerosol can. Do not try to brush on a sealer coat of lacquer type. You can also seal the ghesso with a thin

98

Coat the paper well with more paint to saturate it and cement it down. Apply pressure with brush.

Coat all surfaces of the paper towel thoroughly as you make folds over and inside the framework.

coat of clear varnish. Brush carefully and do not over-brush or it will soften up the gesso. Do not use shellac because it is all but impossible to brush it on without streaking.

You can glaze any gesso before it is completely dry (if no sanding is necessary) or after it is dry if it is one of the water paint types that will soak up paint thinner.

Prepare a glaze of oil or tinting colours, paint thinner and a little oil (just as we did for glazing clear finishes). Brush the glaze on to one surface at a time, working quickly and carefully and following the same direction as the brushing went with the gesso. The more brushing, the more the colour mixes into the gesso. The effect produced is one of solid colour, not a glazed colour over colour.

When this is dry, you can sand it lightly and this will usually cut the tops off the fine ridges of the brush marks. These cut-off ridges will be lighter, thus recovering the glazed antique look.

For a true glazed effect, you must glaze over a dry surface that does not soak up the glaze— either over an oil-base gesso or over a water paint gesso that has first been sealed. Apply

the glaze, brushing it out all that is necessary. Wipe it off if it does not look right and start over. When dry, this, too, can be sanded lightly to emphasize the fine lines of the glaze.

If you glaze, be sure the colour of the gesso is a lighter shade than desired for the finished piece. Also be sure the glaze is the proper colour, so that when coated over or brushed into the gesso, the combination will produce the correct colour.

Texturing gesso: Interesting textures are made by varying the thickness of the gesso so that it will drag or swirl as desired and build up into patterns when you work it with tools of one kind or another.

Dragging a dry brush over partially-set gesso will produce a texture. You can crosshatch, swirl and stipple. Use a spatula, putty knife, fork or comb to run patterns into the gesso. Imitate wood grain by roughly (or skilfully, if you can) copying a grain pattern on to the gesso with a stiff brush, comb or rubber graining tool. Use your imagination here. Make graining and texturing tools by notching pieces of wood or twisting wire into shapes.

99

After the corners are finished, continue around the frame with more towels and paint. Use roller.

Several successive layers of paper can be built up. Finish can be rough-textured or patterned.

Ghesso and paper: You can easily cover flaws, the roughest butt ends of lumber and even open, but firm, joints with paper and ghesso. Apply a coating of water paint ghesso to the raw wood surface. Next lay the paper over the ghesso and press it into place. Then coat the paper with ghesso, either smoothly or with a texture. When dry, this combination is hard and sticks well. Even applied to orange crates, it can make stacks of them look well when they are used for book cases. Paper or cardboard also can be glued to wood first and then coated with ghesso. But be sure the paper is glued firmly.

Ghesso and cloth: You can firm up crates or cheap pieces of cabinetry by wrapping a good strong cloth like duck or linen around the corners and gluing the cloth down well. Then this can be covered with ghesso. Cloth also makes for some fine decorative effects. Burlap glued into door panels and covered with ghesso—though not enough to conceal the cloth weave—makes a handsome textured finish.

Ghesso mixes: In addition to the ghesso materials we have discussed, you can try other combinations and perhaps discover a good formula of your own. You can combine glue, Alabastine, plaster of Paris and any colouring with water paint and an inert filler material that will blend. Also, you can find old ghesso formulas in art books. Some of these require the character of an alchemist to understand, but they are fun to play with.

Some Standard Painted Finishes

Antique white: The simplest version of this popular finish is effected by coating a piece with an off-white paint. Tint the white with yellow ochre, and add a bit of burnt umber as well.

A better antique white is made with a coat of off-white over which an old ivory glaze is added. Prepare the glaze from yellow ochre and burnt umber. Then milk it down with white and brush it over the thoroughly dried off-white. Scuff-sand very lightly with fine paper to achieve a better balance of tone. Shade carvings, mouldings and the like with the same glaze darkened with burnt umber. Finish with a thin coat of flat varnish and rub. Characteristic

This TV cabinet can be given an expensive decorator finish, antique white, with simple materials.

After cleaning all exposed surface of dirt and wax, apply an off-white, oil-base, fast-dry paint.

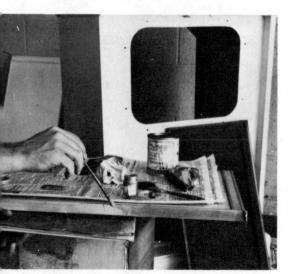

Put on two coats of paint to cover thoroughly. Use thin brush for gold trim on door mouldings.

With a clean brush, apply a nice, smooth antique glaze, working it down until aged tone results.

distress marks and other antiquing effects can be incorporated in the finish. Gold trim can be added. (See Specialty Finishes for further information.)

The finest antique white is produced by adding subtle transparencies over the glaze and distress marks. Milky-tinted, thin varnish, old ivory-tinted varnish and hazy, soft-shadow

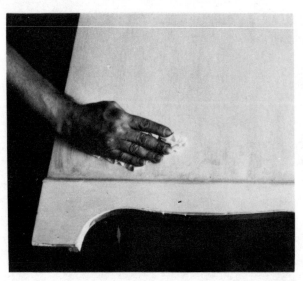

If the glaze doesn't come out right, wipe it off with plenty of paint thinner and try once more.

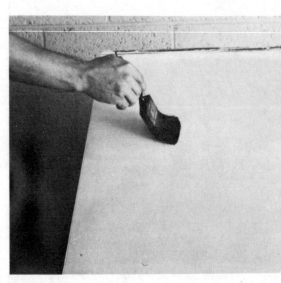

Very light cross brushing with a dry and very soft brush, when glaze is drying, enhances effect.

Shade the legs to relieve the plain cabinetry. Brush on a dark glaze; let it set until tacky.

Wipe away the central area, leaving the colour glaze around the edges. Use clean, lintless rag.

violet—all add an ageing and softening effect.

With walnut or mahogany, open the grain with a wire brush and apply a palomino finish.

Use an off-white as the base coat. Then glaze and fill with the ivory tint.

Ghesso-coated pieces also produce good

102

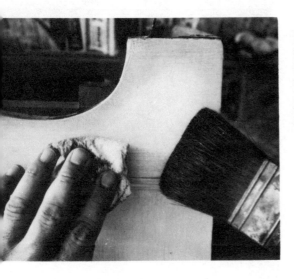

Brush out the glaze, feathering it from darkest edge to lighter inner area. Use cloth for spots.

When dry, the shaded sections can be touched up with fine sandpaper to soften effect as needed.

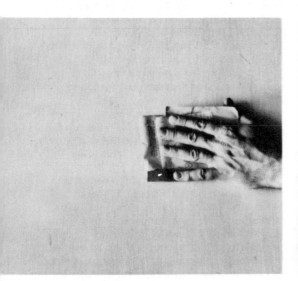

Very light sanding softens the entire glaze on the cabinet. Finish with coat of flat varnish.

Reassemble hardware on the refinished cabinet, preferably with new 'antique finished' screws.

antique whites. Glaze over the ghesso. Where a water-soluble paint type of ghesso is used, you can enhance the beauty of the finish with watery transparencies brushed over the dry ghesso.

French colonial green: This is properly a

This attractive classic table was ghessoed and painted and antiqued in French colonial green.

Even the old oak Christmas tree tables take a new lease of life with a light palomino finish.

ghesso finish. It looks especially well on French and Italian Provincial-styled chests and cabinets. Coat with a light green ghesso and glaze with a chrome green. Antique and age out if desired. Gold trim, if not overdone, will improve the piece.

Fruitwood: Apply a wash coat to produce a pale brown maple tone. Over this, glaze a thin burnt umber. Distress for antique fruitwood. Tones can vary from the soft brown to a more yellowish maple or even to a reddish (burnt sienna) old cherry.

Provincials: These include the fruitwood and related finishes in soft, brownish tones, glazed and shaded. The Italian Provincial pieces look well when they run into the straw tones as well as the brown. Other combinations of colours in the wash coat-glaze or palomino finish work well. Driftwood greys and greens and pickled greys produce a good effect.

Pickled pine: Wash coat knotty pine with a delicate brown which resembles a naturally-aged pine. Glaze with a pickling tone made from raw umber and white, adding yellow ochre or burnt umber for the best final tone.

Oriental lacquer colours: Duplicate a lustrous oriental finish by applying a tinted varnish transparency over a base coat of bril-

liant solid colour. Rub and polish with fine-grade Tri-M-Ite papers (400 to 600), using water for a lubricant. Finish with pumice stone and a rubbing oil made of one part boiled linseed oil and five parts paint thinner.

Feudal oak: Scrub out the grain with a wire brush. Stain with burnt umber. Fill and glaze with a deep brown tone made from black and pure red (not burnt sienna). Add varnish to the glaze to make it a finish coat in itself.

Charcoal: Texture fir or pine with a steel brush. Stain with pure black water-soluble paint reduced with water. When it is dry, brush in a thin white water-soluble paint to get the precise charcoal shade desired. Finish with thin flat varnish or a light spray of lacquer sealer.

Old hickory: Stain with burnt umber and, when dry, sand well to give an aged, varied colouring. Seal, then wash coat with a light, smoky tone. Shade with burnt umber in carvings and mouldings and highlight by sanding off the high spots. Seal sanded spots and then glaze with a tone made from burnt umber and yellow ochre, slightly milked down. Finish with well rubbed flat varnish.

School house red: A palomino. Base coat is bright red. Glaze with black or dark brown, but fill open-grain woods first.

Specialty Finishes

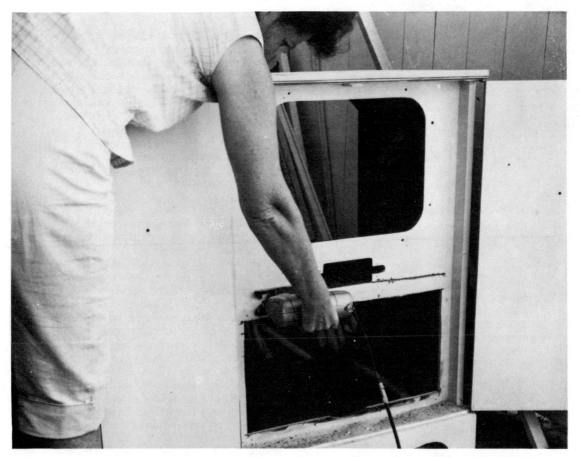

An old TV console is a good subject for experimentation. It will be converted into a utility cabinet.

ALL things considered, the clear finishes are the most difficult of all, the painted finishes are easy and the ghessos are fun. But for an exercise in unbridled creativity that even the kids can enjoy—and often as not come up with superlative originations—the specialty finishes like imitation stone are tops.

All the rules we learned about working with finishing materials (except safety precautions) now are forgotten. Here we combine oil

Piece of scrollwork makes an ideal stencil for spray application on large surfaces of cabinet.

system, water system and shellac system ingredients with almost anything lying around loose. By exploiting the characteristics of materials which make them incompatible for standard finishes, we bend them to our will to produce exotic and fantastic designs and colours.

Here as never before the watchword is *experiment*, with happy disregard for all common sense and rules of mixing paints of all kinds. This is a paradise for the abstract painter and the impressionist. Indeed, you will create far more tasteful and interesting 'paintings' using these methods than any half ton of 'artists' of the slightly unskilled school of paint drippers.

The basic techniques are remarkably simple. Materials include everything you have used for the standard finishes and a few extra things like dried sea horses and metallic thread.

Do not take any formulas or prescriptions

too seriously. They are simply guides to get you started. And do not try too hard to ever duplicate exactly any one finish you achieve. But do enjoy 'open end' finishing in full confidence that every mistake may be the birth of a great idea. And no one will ever know where you went wrong.

Stone and Ceramic Simulation

Marble, gneiss, schist, quartz, and an endless variety of igneous and conglomerate stone effects are wonderfully simple to make. While you can work on large areas such as table tops, the best results are obtained with small squares or rectangles that will be used like real stone or ceramic tile to lay on table tops or use as panels.

Basic materials include bar-top varnish, water-soluble interior wall paint, shellac, metallic powders (gold, bronze, silver) and dry pigment powders (mainly burnt umber, burnt sienna and yellow ochre). These dry powders are obtainable at most paint stores or art stores and come either in small containers or in bulk form and are very inexpensive.

You will need linseed oil, paint thinner, alcohol or methylated spirit, spirit soluble powders and lacquer thinner. Some old brushes come in handy. You can also make good use of tiny coloured glass beads or even the little decorative beadlets used to trim cake. You will use vegetable colourings, coloured metallic or cloth threads, dried seaweed and sea horses, chips of real stone and semi-precious stone, inks—anything that can be embedded in the heavy paint or varnish (like casting in plastic) to produce any effect you can imagine.

Get all your materials in cans and set up on a table where you can get to them as inspiration strikes. A five- or six-inch square of Masonite, plywood or plain board will be just right.

First creative experiment: Remember, we do not wait for anything to dry unless specifically noted. These applications are done while the materials are fresh and wet.

1. Coat the square with white water-soluble paint.

For ceramic pattern, use paint and varnish base then smear on white latex or vinyl flat paint.

With a brush and oil colours, draw veinings into the base coating. Be bold; use irregular strokes.

Mix metallic gold powder in spirit and let it drip from brush or splatter it at the surface.

With a broad putty knife, spread the whole conglomeration around until it looks like marble.

2. Pour unthinned bar-top fast-dry varnish on the board and spread it around.

3. Lift a glob of the paint out of the can (using it thick like ghesso) and, with a stick, drag it around in the varnish to produce marble patterns.

4. Into a small container such as the cap of a bottle, pour methylated spirit and add

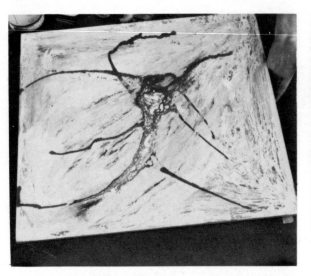

For additional effect, pour any thinned-out colouring material on to surface and let it run free.

To simulate quartz veining, run out thin lines of white glue from squeeze bottle or use brush.

gold metallic powder. With a small artist's brush, dip up the solution and then let it drip on to the varnish and watch it spread out in unusual patterns.

5. Using the brush again, guide some of the thin gold and spirit solution around in the varnish to make gold veins.

6. Splash a little dry pigment powder (yellow ochre or burnt sienna) here and there and spread it with a stick or with an air hose. (A small rubber tube on the valve of an air-filled inner tube works well.)

7. Now use the spirit powders dissolved in spirit to produce other veins and mottled effects to simulate stone.

8. Plain oil pigments in paint thinner can be brushed into the mix. Coloured water-soluble paint will add still more variation.

9. Drop glass beads, etc., into it. Lay coloured thread in it like veins. Press seaweed into it. Press sea horses in. Place tiny shells in it. Put in anything that you wish.

10. Drag the water paint with a brush, stick or putty knife. Spread the colours with

an air hose and small brush. Pick up the board and tilt it this way and that to make the mix run.

11. Let it dry thoroughly.

12. Now it can be used as it is or you can sand it down, cutting through shells, glass and everything as you would grind down semi-precious stone.

13. On this still other layers can be added.

14. Finally, varnish, sand, rub and polish, just as you would for a high-gloss finish, and you'll get the polished stone effect.

Squares made in this way can be laid on any surface, just as you would lay tile. They can be glued down alone, set between strips of wood or combined with ceramic tile.

Experiment freely. Try various colours for base coats and use contrasting colours over them. You can use oil solvent paints and enamels, too. You can spray lacquer colours as a base. You can coat the base with shellac. All these applications produce varying effects—and you probably will never do the same thing twice.

Additional washes, glazes, metallics, etc., can be worked in to produce realistic stone effects.

Close-up of finished board reveals the emulsion effects of the water-soluble additives in varnish.

Close-up of another area might well be part of an abstract painting or photo of a lava flow.

Black-and-white picture does not do justice to the brilliant colours obtained by paint mixing.

Gold Pool

Paint or lacquer any wood surface a forest green or one of the olive shades. When this is dry, brush clear water over the surface (with

the surface horizontal). Into the water, drop a small amount of dry pigment powder (burnt umber or raw umber). Spread this with a brush. It will require a little time because the powder does not want to combine with the water. Do not use water-soluble powders; use the standard oil-soluble type.

When you have spread the dry powder in the water so that it generally covers the area, drip a mixture of gold metallic powder and spirit freely into the water and powder mix. This spirit and gold will spread in a whirlpool fashion, forming generally circular patterns. Drip the gold-spirit mix in until you have completely covered the surface with these circles of gold.

Let the piece sit where it is, keeping it as level as possible to avoid run-off until the water

To simulate volcanic rocks, use spirit-soluble powder dyes such as mahogany, brown maple, etc.

Covered with a ceramic finish coated with spar varnish, old metal table enlivens back patio.

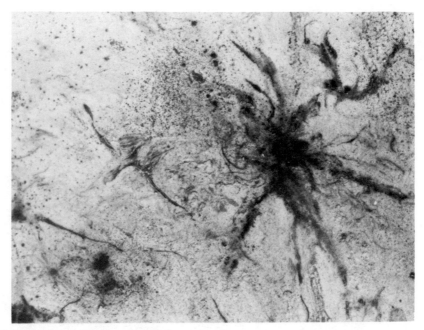

Detail of table top shows broad and simple patterns to use on large surfaces.

Working the mass of colours and materials generally from top to bottom produces a rock pattern.

and spirit have dried, leaving pools of gold flakes with borders of dry powder around them. Next spray this lightly with lacquer sealer. If you used lacquer as the base coat, you can then spray lacquer sealer freely for a thicker finish. If you used paint, spray only a light coat to seal in the gold and pigment powder. Over this lacquer sealer, finish with lacquer (if a lacquer base coat) or varnish (if a paint base coat).

This whirlpool effect is excellent for door panels and other decor. Add burnished brass trim to the piece for a most handsome and masculine finish, ideal for a man's executive desk.

Drop and Emulsion Effects

Dripping spirit with colour and dropping other mixtures into a wet finish, or on a dry finish, will produce many possible finishes.

111

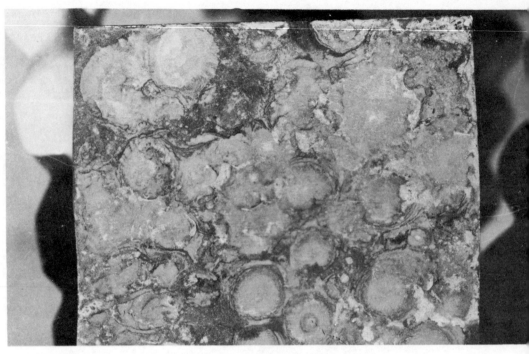

Eye-catching gold pattern is obtained by dripping big globs of solution on surface from above.

Experiment, using all the finishing materials. Use the several kinds of pigments in their proper solvents and in solvents they do not normally mix with.

1. Prepare a base colour and apply it to the surface. While wet, or when dry, drip colours mixed in varnish, shellac, methylated spirit, oil, water, etc., on to the surface.

2. Spray, roll on or brush a clear, translucent or semi-opaque coating over this when dry.

An infinite variety of patterns will result from the many mixtures of pigments and solvents or just wet solutions. You will find that certain of these repeat their patterns so that you can control the designs.

But what good are words for such an open-end kind of creativity? Experiment with art and finishing colours and finishes and solvents. Create your own special effects and guard the secret formulas.

Metallic Powders

There is one way and one way only to apply the gold, brass, bronze and silver metallic powders to trim larger surfaces properly. Do not brush it on, wipe it on. The powdery, cheap look resulting from brushing gold powder mixed with any liquid usable on to wood is usually more detracting than attractive. Even sprayed metallics such as are available in aerosol cans do not look like real metal. But try it this way and see the difference:

1. Coat the surface with unthinned shellac. Coat it lightly, but coat it completely.

112

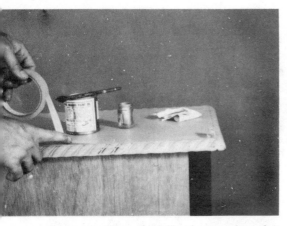

To prevent spillover of metallic trim to nearby surface, cover latter with ¾-inch masking tape.

Prepare trim by coating small section at a time with 4-lb. unthinned shellac. Use a thin brush.

With dry, soft brush, splash the metallic powder on to the still wet surface. Do not paint it on.

With a small cloth or leather pad, dry-burnish the metallic powder gently into the wet shellac.

2. Splash some gold powder from the container or drip it on with a brush or stick.

3. Using a small flat pad made from hard cloth or leather, rub the gold powder over the surface, and rub it well to burnish it smooth.

That is all there is to it. One look and you will know the vast difference, for this application produces a surface so close to real metal, or leaf, that you can hardly tell it from the real thing.

Glazing (or shading) the gold or brass produces a fine effect. For example, after wiping a light gold or brass on to a picture frame, wipe a glaze of a little raw umber over it and rub it down well to get a burnished brass look. Burnt sienna over gold produces the red gold patina. Burnt umber will age it.

Wiping gold, silver or such on to a board and then applying a ceramic or stone finish produces an exciting gold quartz or black gold effect.

Another idea: On a wiped gold surface, drip

Work with a fold of paper or piece of cardboard to catch any overflow when applying the powder.

With care, shade the gold trim with burnt umber; work it into all the depressions of the moulding.

After wiping the shading pigment down well, carefully brush on a thin glaze over all; let it dry.

Finished trim appearance closely resembles that of gold leaf without gritty look of gold paint.

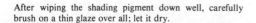

a mixture of gold powder and spirit and let it dry out well before spraying it lightly with lacquer sealer. This very delicately mottles the gold and gives it an excellent aged appearance.

To create a Venetian gold effect, apply white ghesso to a picture frame and sand it with fine paper until very smooth. Then coat the ghesso with burnt sienna colour. Mix a little varnish with the pigment to make it stick and give a hard surface. When dry, cover with wiped-on gold. When this is dry, carefully sand and scrape the surface to expose bits of the red and

the ghesso white for that old Venetian gold look.

Texturing Wood Surfaces

Picture frames are particularly attractive when the wood is textured. This is done by sandblasting, steel brushing, tooling or by applying a heavy coat of ghesso and texturing it while it is wet.

Soft wood like pine can be scrubbed with a stiff steel brush to yield a combed texture (ridges and grooves). Palomino finishes take well on such a surface. Wood also can be hammered, rough-carved or scratched to get texture effects.

With ghesso, even plywood and Masonite can take on an entirely new character. Coat the surface with a thick application of fast-dry interior paint (after draining off the solvent). A piece of wood that is notched, a rubber graining tool, an old stiff bristle brush, a coarse burlap rag—these and numerous 'around the house' articles can be used to produce patterns in the ghesso. Dragging a brush in it as it begins to set up or working it the same way with a notched (saw-tooth) stick can produce patterns that give the appearance of sandblasted wood.

Glazing colour over this textured surface and then wiping it off the top, or sanding it off, will produce a palomino shaded and highlighted effect.

You can use a saw blade like a scraper to comb softwood to produce ridges or you can file teeth of many shapes into a strip of metal and use this as a comb for the raw wood or for the ghesso. Kitchen tools like graters, potato mashers and biscuit cutters all make fine tools for texturing ghesso and add considerable interest to the process.

Crackled Finishes

The perverse nature of man is such that the same crackling that ruins a good paint job in time or a wrong enamel job suddenly is much desired for decorative finishes.

As silly as it seems to want to do such a thing, the effect is quite handsome. Crackled antique white with old gold worked into the crackle or a powder blue crackle over gold or white will make your status-climbing neighbour tremble with repressed envy.

To crackle a finish, we must make the coat of paint shrink and slip over a surface so that it breaks up into small, more or less regular patterns. Physics and chemistry take care of the regularity of pattern, based on the law of shrinkage (like mud in the hot sun). We will formulate materials to give them a chance to shrink.

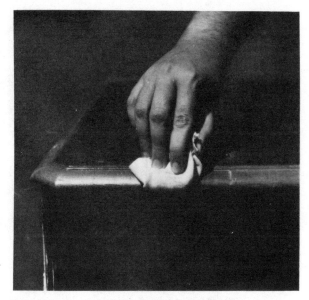

Burnishing operation is simpler with plain moulding than with fancy. Be generous with the powder.

Coat a surface with fast-drying varnish taken directly from the can without thinning. As it begins to set up tack-free after about five or ten minutes, brush on a coat of water-soluble interior paint. Watch the water paint spread out into lace patterns if the varnish is not quite set enough. When a little drier, the coating of water paint will take so that you can actually brush it on to the still fresh varnish. Then, as the water paint dries out before the varnish does, it will separate, producing fine crackle lines. When all is thoroughly dry, you can glaze and top coat, if desired, with clear varnish.

Gloss enamel that is fast-drying can be used in place of varnish. You might find other materials to produce varied crackle effects. Be sure the undercoating is slippery and slower-drying than the top coating.

To get a two-colour crackle effect, first paint the surface any colour. Then, when it is dry, coat it with varnish and paint the crackle coat

115

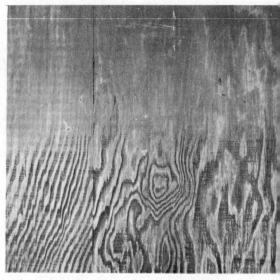

To texture soft wood, use a stiff wire brush and scrub first against the grain and then with it.

This shows the difference between the raw wood, top, and the section textured with a wire brush.

Entire board has been given a base coat of light colour. This is lost on untextured centre section.

Inexpensive wood can be given expensive-looking grain line if worked over with paint brush comb.

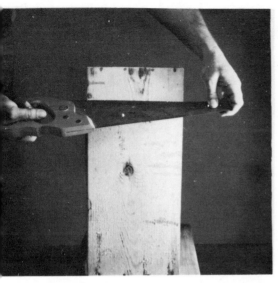

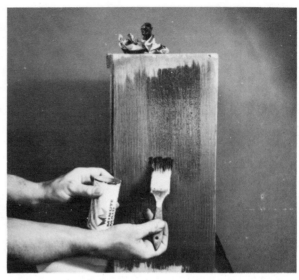

Very low grade wood used for fruit crates can be comb-grained effectively with a short, sharp saw.

Sand lightly, then coat the striated crate wood with a base colour. When dry, apply a plain glaze.

Wipe the glaze across the grain so that it will load up in the striations. This heightens effect.

Similar effects can be had on cheaper grades of mahogany plywood. Remember, comb with grain.

117

The crackle effect simulating old age in furniture is widely combined with the ever popular 'antique white' finishes.

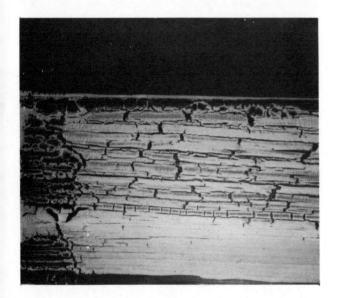

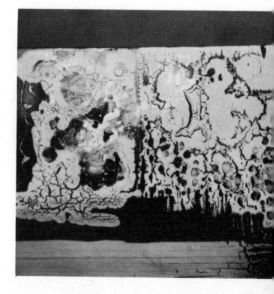

Samples of typical crackle effects. *Left:* More or less even parallel lines, broken up. *Right:* These are almost like the abstract paintings which are to be seen in many of the avant-garde exhibitions.

This is what happens when the water-soluble flat paint, used in crackle effects, is put on over the varnish base coat too soon. It doesn't combine well.

over that. Or, use just the crackle coat and allow it to dry. Then, give it a thin coat of varnish and, when it is dry, rub, brush or wipe oil colour or another paint on it, leaving it in the crackle lines only. You may slightly glaze all for a fine crackled palomino effect.

Do not try too seriously to copy one of your own crackles unless you have a completely insensitive nervous system. This is a most frustrating experience. Crackle finishes are unique and are partly your creation, partly the paint's and partly nature's. It's a one-of-a-kind creative experience. You can produce similar patterns but will never match one exactly.

Note that lacquer or lacquer thinner applied wet to varnish or paint will wrinkle it, not crackle it, unless the under surface is slippery enough for the finish to slide as it shrinks.

Antique Effects (Distressing)

Now that you have learned how to restore a piece, let's work out how to almost ruin one—but neither too much nor too little, so it will have that fine old hand-rubbed, much-used, well-preserved, authentic antique look that will

With a little more waiting, the paint binds a little better on the varnish, but not enough to crackle in the proper manner.

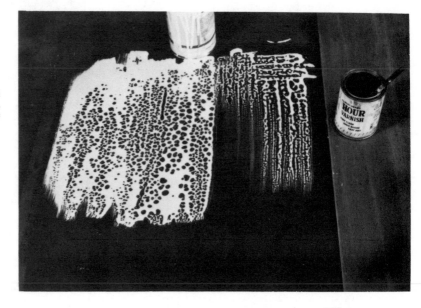

119

Applied when the varnish has formed a slight skin over its entire surface, paint now crackles well.

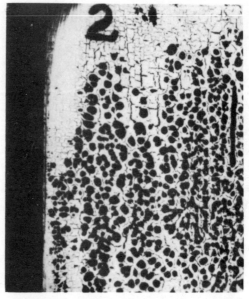

With a little experimentation, it is possible to produce a considerable variety of crackle effects.

confuse and dismay those who think they inherited all the fine old pieces.

Distressing is the word. The distressed finish is the antique finish. Some unknown fine old finisher came up with that word to describe antique finishing, and today it is the normal trade expression.

Factories that specialize in antique reproductions use lengths of chain, old cinders, hammers, nails, piano wire, drills, ashes and chemicals. They bury the wood in special muds and clays, they bake it and they soak it in sun and rain. They wear it down on the edges, stain it with ink and then splatter it with synthetic fly specks. All those little dots so popular on furniture today are supposed to be fly specks. Who would even think of having an antique fruitwood dining table without those little black dots all over it?

Scratch the wood, paint scratches on it, beat it, kick it, pour vinegar on it, dump some bleach on it in spots or roll it around in the ash pile. Soak it with crankcase oil; tie the dog to it

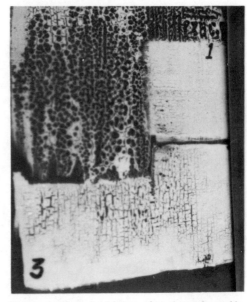

Exposure to the sun is tricky way of opening up the crackle patterns. Compare these photos.

120

Simulated fly specks are easy to make. Using a somewhat dry paint, snap the brush bristles with a finger. For variously-sized dots and patterns, vary distance from the work.

for a few days. Then let it bleach out in sunshine and rain for a month or so. After that, refinish it—but do not repair or patch it!

If this seems a little too much—and it probably is for most—there are easier ways:

1. Fly specks. Make a thick paint of dark brown from oil pigment or from plain paint, or use thick, coloured lacquer. Using a stiff bristle brush, such as a sash brush, dip the tip in, wipe it off on a wood plate and then use your finger to snap the bristles and send flecks of paint flying. Practice, a good sighting eye and some finger coordination will achieve excellent patterns, suggesting a most unusual variety of flies of all sizes.

2. Standard distress marks. Simply paint on little scratch lines with an artist's brush and dark paint, usually burnt or raw umber. Lightly, pray! Too much, too thick does not bring off the idea at all.

3. 'Authentic' distressing. Either in a wood that is to be finished in a clear coat or in the painted coat of an antique white, for example, scratch lines instead of painting them. Use a small, round pointed tool (like an old ball-point pen) and mark up the surfaces just as though Uncle Luke and Aunt Yetta had worked it over for decades. When you glaze the surface, the marks will take the colour. Wipe it off the surface well, leaving the colour in the marks only.

4. Antique white and other painted finishes. A very little wrinkle here and there looks well. Get this wrinkle by painting lacquer in areas you want to age, but just a little.

5. Wipe dark shading colour into crevices, around legs and the like.

6. Sand down rungs of chairs where a child's shoes would have worn them.

'Distress' marks, standard on most antique finishes, can be drawn in by hand with a fine brush. Practise first on old scraps of wood; use leftover cans of paint in odd colours.

After one or two layers of ghesso have been applied, sand down smoothly with fine paper.

Seal the ghesso coat with white shellac, and apply coat of opaque burnt sienna oil paint.

When thoroughly dry, coat the burnt sienna with shellac, in advance of gold burnishing.

Scatter fine gold or brass powder on to the wet shellac. Clean paper below catches any spillover.

7. Most of the things mentioned at the opening of this section actually can be done. Staining, hammering, rolling in cinders, using ashes, vinegar, sun bleaching and the like—all help to give that 'fine old look' to the wood.

8. Multiple glazes and transparencies applied over painted finishes give an aged look. Over a French colonial green, for example, apply a very light coat of amber or aged yellow in a transparency. Over this transparent glaze, still more glazes can go. Use the colours that mean aged: dirty yellows, old, musty greys, rotted browns and the like.

You can 'spill' a little water or tinted—

Burnish the gold (or the brass) to a smooth, bright metallic finish with small, dry cloth pad.

Glaze overall with a burnt umber, applied pure from the can, and then wipe it down with pad.

Seal glaze with shellac. Scrape with small chisel to expose varied colours of the ghesso beneath.

Finished 'antique' picture frame might have come from ancient gallery, will fool experts.

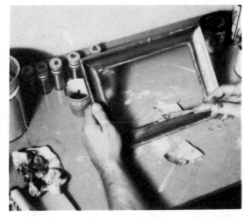

delicately tinted—spirit and let it dry to produce gentle stains. Indeed, if you brush tinted water over the paint and then possibly add a touch of tinted spirit by dripping it into the water, you will get some connoisseur distressing. And for that final, absolutely convincing touch, burn a few spots with an old cigar, pipe ashes or a cigarette.

With all this done, you will have a wonderful piece to use as you start over at the beginning of this book and learn how to repair and refinish. So, in any event, nothing is lost. The finisher goes in circles, restoring a piece for one, only to wind up distressing the same piece when it is given away to someone for Christmas.

Some Unusual Finishes

Dens, playrooms, bars, patios, all deserve an occasional touch of the wild and wonderful. Here are a few ideas:

Sun-baked Western

This is great for a garden that is really lived in. Old oak dining tables and chairs or the old hickory furniture and the like that has the solid, he-man, western tavern and saloon look are made for this finish.

1. Do not strip the old finish off.
2. Scuff-sand and clean off any grease, oil or wax.
3. Use exterior paint for outdoor furniture, interior paint for pieces to be used inside.
4. To white paint, add tinting colours to get light, bleached, desert and sage tones: purple grey, sage grey-green, light sand, pale hazy blue or faded rose. Use only colours you can make by milking down the basic furniture colours: yellow ochre, raw sienna, burnt sienna, burnt umber and raw umber plus a touch of blue to make greens and bluegreys.

All soft, milked-out tones (like bleached paint) are used. Just go ahead and paint the furniture with these colours in various combinations. Use some of the pure, richer colour for trim. After a first base coat, glaze on other colours around carvings or mouldings. Use flat paint to avoid any shine. Umbers wiped into cracks and checks add an interesting touch. Decorate as desired with touches of red, blue, green and yellow.

Let this furniture bleach out in strong summer sunshine. Then wash it down with a light bleaching solution, using a household bleach. Presto! You have that old, sun-drenched, faded look they can't quite get on colour TV and are afraid of in colour western films.

Gay Nineties

To capture the spirit of this fun-loving period,

it is best to first find some colour pictures from magazines, often as not in advertisements.

Here we will use bright strong reds and blues and greens, frills, scrolls, fancy patterns, checks and stripes. Illustrations of needlework from the period give fine ideas for designs. Wallpapers copied from this period serve well for panels on chests. And use lots of trim! Bright, brassy trim.

Plain furniture can be niftied up with carvings, scroll work, 'bead' trim, little spires and curlicues and rosettes. Also, the imitation stone and ceramic finishes go well with the mood for use on table tops and tops of small stands or commodes.

Stencil and Spray

Stencils made from cardboard or wood or scroll work screens of thin plywood, such as are now commonly available in stores supplying materials for the home craftsman, can be used skilfully to produce interesting patterns on otherwise common-place pieces.

Over a solid base coat, spray a very light toner through the grillwork to give a slightly out-of-focus effect. When the pattern is applied, then go over all, hazing it in. Wrought iron work, metal chairs, wicker and basket work all can be used for stencils.

Instant Oriental Screen Panels

Cover a panel with wiped-on gold. Dip a wire or nail into ink or other colouring liquid. Aim an air hose down the nail to blow the dye off the wire and on to the panel. A quick blast will produce thistle-like patterns. Then chase the colour out in designs with the air hose. Cover a gold panel in this manner, adding a spot or two of bright colour to get a blossom design; then glaze with a very delicate tone of burnt umber to age it out and you have a screen that will astound most people. If you do not have an air compressor, you will still be able to provide the necessary air pressure by using a beach ball or by attaching a short length of rubber tubing to any inflatable item you own.

Potpourri

An honourable but weathered metal set will serve handsomely for many years if properly repainted.

ANY of the finishes discussed can be applied to outdoor wood furniture, but to protect the finish against weather, a good quality outdoor (marine) spar or polyurethane varnish should be used in place of regular or bar-top varnish.

If you use any of the interior paints for special effects or the like, be sure to add a final coat of clear spar or polyurethane varnish to protect them. Deck enamels and outdoor paints can be used as well for painted finishes. Outdoor furniture should be coated with spar or polyurethane varnish on all surfaces to seal the wood against weathering.

Metal outdoor and indoor furniture can be given any of the painted finishes after first coating with a metal primer. The ceramic and stone finishes work very well to bring fresh life to old metal tables. Just be sure the varnish you use is a spar varnish.

Let's beautify our patios and gardens with colourful finishes. In place of the drab plain wood furniture and so-called 'outdoor furniture', why not the same kind of cabinets and tables you use in the living room? This furniture, finished in bright and unusual painted effects and coated overall with spar varnish, will turn your patio into a paradise and give elegance to the garden.

Pianos: The simplest restoration for a grimy, dark old upright is a bright specialty paint finish such as a crackled antique white with gold trim. You don't have to haul the old monster out of the house. You don't have to strip it. You can lay down tarpaulin or paper and paint it. You don't even have to take it apart, but whatever pieces come off easily can just as well be removed and done outside.

Clean the old varnish with lacquer thinner. When this is dry, give the entire old finish a treatment of oil (1 part) and paint thinner (3 parts). To this add a little varnish. This will soak into the old finish and wake it up enough to be usable as a base for a new paint coat.

You may find, happily or otherwise, depending on your own attitude about upright pianos, that this treatment brings up the old finish. If so, go ahead and give it more treatment until it looks like new. Then top it off with a few thin coats of brushed bar-top varnish.

Suppose you decide to paint. After one application of the renovator, let it dry and apply the paint coats. Do not use a water-soluble paint without first testing it. The chances are that it will not stick. Remember that the lighter colours tend to reduce the size of an object; darker colours make it more conspicuous.

It is also possible to strip a piano in the

The materials for refinishing outdoor furniture are standard: paints, varnish, thinner, brushes.

Start preparing a wooden table by working it over with a stiff wire brush to remove redwood stain.

Less back-bending is necessary if the table is propped vertically. This brushing opens up grain.

Coat the clean wood with stain made of oil pigments blended with linseed oil and paint thinner.

house. Spinets, however, are very little trouble to move out to the garage. If you are going to strip the old finish, take the removable parts of the piano off the main frame and lay them out for easy work.

Using several layers of newspaper or masking paper and some masking tape, completely mask off all the strings, keys, etc.

Strip as you would strip anything else, but know this: old piano finishes were extraordinarily heavy and difficult to handle. The newer spinets often have little or nothing on them.

Children's furniture takes on a wonderland magic when decorated in bright, fanciful colours and designs. The circus theme never grows old with kids. Brilliant reds, blues, yellows and greens with garish brassy trim will delight them.

But children also love to chew on such excit-ing finishes. To protect them from possible toxic effects in some paints and finishes, observe the following precautions:

1. No lead paints. The lead is found primarily in white oil paints and can be fatal.

2. No lacquers or quick finishes.

3. Do use varnishes made from alkyds.

4. Do use enamels made from alkyds with nontoxic colouring dyes.

5. When in doubt about any paint or clear finish, consult your doctor about the ingredients listed on the can.

Antiques: Valuable furniture deserves the craftsmanship of expert restorers. If you are considering the restoration of a Louis XV table or a Sheraton chest, call in an expert.

Antique furniture should be restored to its original condition in terms of sound cabinetry,

127

After letting stained wood dry for several days, cover it all over generously with spar or polyurethane varnish.

She doesn't think the job is so hot? Hand her a brush, let her touch up to her own satisfaction.

colour and finish. The Venus di Milo may look fine without arms, but a sideboard without legs or a chest without drawers does not have quite the same charm.

Do not attempt to restore any pieces of value. But if you have some average pieces such as the commodes or chairs of the 1880's and since, and wish to try your hand on a restoration, go ahead.

First of all, do not scrape or sand any good antique pieces. Preservation of the character of the wood is basic to the art of antique restoration. While it is not always possible to avoid sanding, only a professional is capable of restoring the wood—after sanding—to proper condition.

Do not use any nails on antique furniture. All the repair must be done with glue. Fill the holes and other flaws with wood filler and touch up these patches with hand painted grain, not scratch graining. The filler will not damage the piece in case you find you have a valuable treasure on your hands and later wish to have it restored properly.

Do not bleach the wood. Do not darken it when you stain or colour tone. The very safest procedure is to coat the wood after stripping with a thin application of clear white shellac.

This will protect the wood surface. Over this you may glaze and shade for colour without risking any damage. Finish it off with one thin coat of varnish.

Oil-resin is the classic finish of past centuries but, once applied to the wood, is extremely difficult to get out. Because of its nature, oil-resin will darken many old woods. Here again, it requires professional skill to restore a valuable piece to the proper finish.

In a case where you are sure the piece is of no great value, then by all means use the oil-resin finish, colour toning and very light staining to achieve the finished results you want. You cannot lose on it.

128

To clean metal furniture, use a wire brush and 'Scotch-Brite'. Get rid of all loose rust, paint.

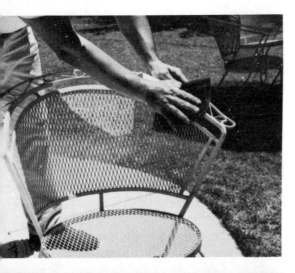

After making sure all rust spots are now shiny bright, cover all bare metal with metal primer.

The spray can is a great time saver here. Use a good grade of lacquer enamel or spar-type enamel.

129

In working on door panel, first wet down surface with water, then apply wax with circular motion.

Lightly scuff-buff the dried wax with a Scotch-Brite ultrafine pad. This levels it off evenly.

Above: Check marks, cracks and splits are simulated by cutting the wood surface open with a thin knife.

Left: Deliberate marring or 'distressing' of wood for an antique effect can be done with small gouge.

A rock rolled over the wood and lightly pounded in produces variety of genuine-looking age marks.

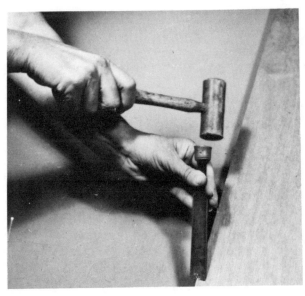

An old table does not have clean, sharp edges. With chisels, chop into wood for antique effect.

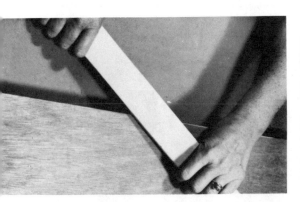

Burnish edges with a piece of smooth hardwood. Press down hard, and handle it like a big file.

Old stains can be reproduced with such household liquids as vinegar, coffee, tea, iodine, ink, etc.

There is a French polish cult that should be avoided in the interest of preserving fine furniture. This groups holds to the weird delusion that the shiny French polish is the proper and only finish for furniture. If you can find one such follower who so much as knows when French polish was invented, then that finisher might be knowledgeable enough to be trusted with good pieces.

French polish is nothing more than shellac

Another ageing process: Rubbing burnt umber over distress marks and then wiping it down strongly.

Junk lamps lend themselves readily to rejuvenation. First step is to remove all grease and dirt.

which is applied with a pad and a lubricant—usually an oil or spirit, depending on the 'secret' formula of the finisher. This method of applying an extremely glossy and perfectly even coating to furniture has limited use only. The oil-resin coating, applied with a pad, produces as glossy a finish as is humanly possible. But shellac, while inferior in most ways

If lamp base is metal, prime with metal primer. If wood or pottery, seal it with white shellac.

Apply moderately thick unthinned varnish as a base for a crackle finish or ceramic colourings.

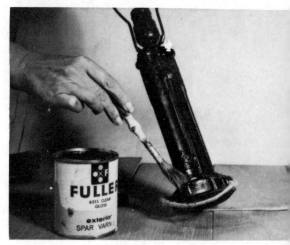

Old tables are favourite objects of all furniture refinishers. First step in revamping is sanding.

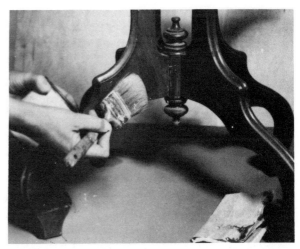

Clean off dust from sandpapering. Seal the old finish with clear shellac, scuff sand when dry.

to oil-resin, is faster and easier to build up, so it became fashionable at one time, just as fast finishes are popular today among those who do not like to pay for quality.

All of which is to say that antique furniture deserves the same care and respect we give to old paintings, glass, pottery and such. Protect it with shellac, but do not carve it or saw it up or pound nails into it.

To enhance crackle effect, add stains, metallic powder, or let coloured paint dribble down sides.

Tint a water-soluble interior fast-dry paint to desired colour and brush a thick layer on base.

133

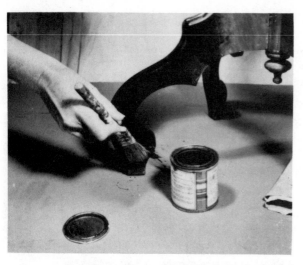

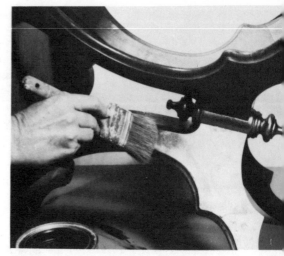

For a fine crackle, coat wood with varnish tinted a dark green. Colour will show through the lines.

Carvings and moulded edges usually need treatment with a small flat brush. Daub well into cracks.

When varnish has set slightly, brush on crackle coat of green interior-type water-soluble paint.

For that aged look, stain the paint with alcohol, vinegar or water, but be careful not to overdo.

Waxing finished surfaces: For a fine, smooth wax finish that has a softer lustre than that obtained by merely spraying on a one-operation type wax or buffing, use the following technique:

Dampen a soft cloth. Wet the finish before applying wax. Work a good quality paste wax into the wet cloth and lightly wipe it on to the surface, using a little whirlpool stroke, until the entire area is covered. As you apply the wax on

For a nice touch, finish the edges of the table with metallic gold. Rub in well with cloth pad.

As a final protective coat, brush on thinned out flat varnish. Then scour with Scotch-Brite pads.

To preserve the deliberately distressed finish of the table, wipe down with glaze of antique colour.

Children's furniture can be used from one generation to another if strengthened and refinished.

the wetted finish, you will see at once where wax is covering and where more must be wiped on.

Allow the wax to dry for a half hour or so. Now use an ultrafine Scotch-Brite pad (as you would use fine steel wool) to level off the wax. Rubbing lightly, very lightly, stroke in the direction of the grain on clear finishes or with the longer length of the surface on painted finishes. This light rubbing will cut off the irregular

Rockers are always popular. If bottom pieces are worn, strengthen with new strips, screwed down.

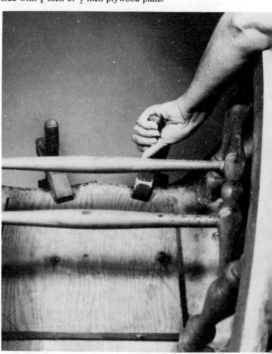

Rungs loose? Pack these openings with slivers of veneer and good glue. Wipe away excess with rag.

If cane seat shows signs of collapse, reinforce from underside with $\frac{1}{8}$ inch or $\frac{1}{2}$ inch plywood plate.

ridges of the wax, leaving the coating very smooth and level. Just as fine finish sanding levels off a finish to produce a soft lustrous patina, so does the light rubbing of wax achieve a patina that is much less garish than unrubbed wax.

Follow this operation by buffing lightly with a soft cloth. At no time is it necessary to use any muscle. Do not rub hard. The hand rubbing so often thought necessary with wax only is a difficult way to level off the wax. Cutting it with the abrasive pad does the same job with a minimum of effort.

If you use a good wax like paste Simoniz and apply two thin coats in this manner, under normal usage you need wax no more than two to three times a year. In between, use only a damp dust cloth to clean the wax or, if necessary, use a little soap with the water. A heavy wax surface built up on furniture accomplishes nothing.

Touch-up of Furniture

Clear finishes: Materials: Flat and gloss water clear lacquer; tinting colours; small artist's brushes; lacquer thinner; wood filler or grain filler; 400 and 600 Wet-or-Dry Tri-M-Ite

136

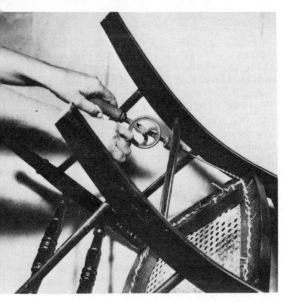

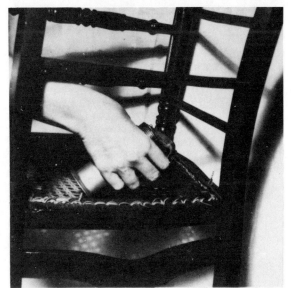

Wobbly joints are common. To get glue into them, drill small holes, about $\frac{3}{16}$ inch, partly through.

Force glue in from squeeze bottle container or, better, from pressure-type oil can, free of oil.

To clean but not remove a finish, use denatured shellac solvent diluted with a little cold water.

paper; Scotch-Brite ultrafine pad or 0000 steel wool; a small, flat carving chisel.

Cigarette burns and other deep or discolouring damage: Cut away the disfigured wood. Fill carefully with surfacing filler coloured closely to match the finish, but make this tone of colour lighter than the finish.

Level off the filler with 400 Wet-or-Dry paper, using no lubricant. Use the paper in a small piece, working carefully so as not to cut through surrounding finish.

Now, using the tinting colours, a small brush and lacquer (or lacquer sanding seal), mix small quantities of colour by dipping the brush into lacquer thinner first, then into the pigments, and blending it into the lacquer or sanding sealer. By dipping the brush into lacquer thinner, reduce the mixture thin enough to brush easily and smoothly. Paint in grain marks that follow the grain of the wood on either side of the flaw.

Apply over this a clear coat of sealer or lacquer, using a small flat brush about half an inch wide so that you can lay a thin coat on in one or two quick passes. Avoid any unnecessary brushing.

137

Tone to match the finish by applying very thin coatings of lacquer tinted with the colour. Over this apply a few coats of clear lacquer mixed from the gloss and flat to match the finish lustre. These coats can be applied more thickly and, after each coat is dry, more can be added to build up the depression to a perfectly level surface. Sand the spot with Wet-or-Dry Tri-M-Ite paper, using water as a lubricant. Sand carefully until level. Rub with a pad of steel wool or Scotch-Brite for the final matching lustre.

Clear lacquer or sanding sealer can be used to fill, coat by coat, any flaw that does not require colour toning.

Fill scratches by building with sanding sealer and then working level.

Painted finishes: Fill depressions if necessary with wood filler and then, using colour to match the finish, carefully paint over the spot, feathering into the old finish. Work it down to level it off and match the lustre.

Lacquer sanding sealer and lacquer (commercial spray type) is used because it dries fast, builds up well and is easily worked. It is used on all kinds of old clear finishes with the exception of a very few rare synthetics. In any case, where lacquer cannot be used, substitute shellac and varnish.

Oil finishes: Patch with wood surfacing filler. Grain with a chisel and by wiping an oil glaze over the spot to darken the grain imitation. Tone with flat oil and colour to match.

Guide to Materials

Abrasives: Use only fine cabinet papers on the wood surfaces, cabinet finishing papers for dry sanding of finishes and Tri-M-Ite Wet-or-Dry papers for wet sanding of fine finishes. Cabinet finishing papers generally have a garnet or an aluminium oxide cutting surface. Do not make the mistake of using ordinary flint sandpaper.

Pumice stone and rottenstone are also used for rubbing down a finish to an extra fine smoothness. They are especially useful on a varnish finish. Pumice stone is a type of volcanic glass which is powdered for use as an abrasive. It comes in eight grades from coarse to fine, though the four finest grades are generally used to rub a varnish finish. The rottenstone is a type of limestone which is finer still than the pumice stone. Both are available in packages of one pound or more at your local paint supply stores.

Most often, the pumice stone and rottenstone are used in succession on the final coat of varnish. The pumice stone is sprinkled on the surface and then rubbed with a felt pad which has been dipped in a lubricant such as water or rubbing oil. The pad should be kept wet throughout so that the pumice is not rubbed dry, the rubbing pressure should be light and the strokes should always be made with the grain of the wood. When the surface is smooth to the touch, the pumice is removed completely with water and a soft cloth. This produces a soft finish, but the highest gloss is produced by using the rottenstone with a felt pad and a lubricant in the same manner. When the job is finished, the rottenstone is also flushed with water. If oil has been used as a lubricant, it is also removed, chamois being the best for this.

Rubbing pads and compounds: Steel wool has been a standby in the past. The comparatively new Scotch-Brite pads in two grades, utility and ultrafine, are far superior to any steel wool for all furniture finishing. Cost is much lower due to the durability of the pads; they do not splinter or break up like wool when used with removers and other liquids. Compounds on the market are generally usable and any name brand product can be used.

Varnishes and enamels: Reputable name brand products long established are all adequate. A line of varnishes often includes a range of clear coatings from flat to high gloss that are fast drying and alcohol proof and handle well.

Paints: Oil-base paints supplied by several old established firms under name brands are all adequate. They vary in their characteristics. Select the paint that you find best for you. The water-soluble interior paints vary considerably in their working characteristics.

138

Above: With artist's brush, carefully touch up light spots. *Below:* Protective coat of thinned varnish can be brushed on or wiped on with rag.

Right: When clear finish is dry, rub down gently with Scotch-Brite pad. Do not press too hard.

Patching compounds: Cellulose fillers, grain fillers, Alabastine, plastic wood stopping, and others are unsurpassed for our work.

Paint removers and solvents: Several name brand products of both liquid and paste type work well. The liquid types sold in gallon and larger quantities for commercial work, rather than the more expensive types marketed chiefly to the hobbyist, are to be preferred. Avoid use of the removers which are designed to be flushed from the surface with water.

Lacquer: Again, the established name brand firms supply fine lacquers. Often as not in larger towns local firms also supply excellent materials. For the finest lacquers, lacquer enamels and lacquer tinting colours, the automotive lacquers are far superior in all respects. While the comparable price per quart or gallon is higher, the final cost is no more because they go much farther.

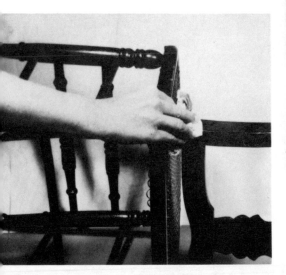

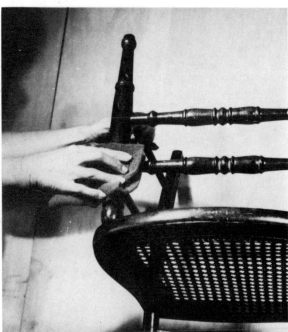

139

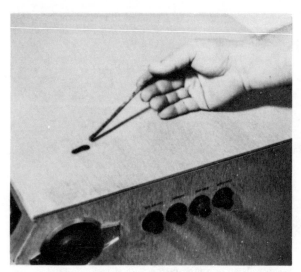

Cigarettes often leave nasty marks on TV cabinets, and are especially bad on light woods.

Only treatment is to cut out burned area. Use a sharp knife and try not to enlarge damage.

Left: Patch hole with a cellulose filler or plastic wood lighter in colour than cabinet wood. Fill depression evenly.

Below: Paint in grain strokes to match cabinet finish. A magnifying glass is required for the job.

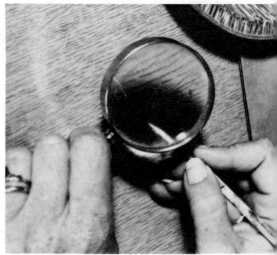

With as few strokes as possible, coat the repaired area with lacquer sealer and lacquer finish.

Complete patching job with delicate wet sanding with 600 Tri-M-Ite paper between lacquer coats.

WU9